To Bill

God Love You,

Father "T."

CHRIST
in Catechesis

Giving the Whole Christ to the Whole Person

by the Daughters of St. Paul

ST. PAUL EDITIONS

NIHIL OBSTAT:
  Rev. Richard V. Lawlor, S.J.
  Censor
IMPRIMATUR:
  ✣ Most Rev. Thomas V. Daily
  September 30, 1983

Library of Congress Cataloging in Publication Data

Main entry under title:
Christ in catechesis.

  Includes bibliographies.
  1. Catechetics—Catholic Church. 2. Christian education—Philosophy. 3. Catholic Church—Doctrines. I. Daughters of St. Paul.
  BX1968.C47   1983   207   83-18826
  ISBN 0-8198-1432-6
       0-8198-1433-4 (pbk.)

Grateful acknowledgement is made to the following publishers for their kind permission to quote passages from copyrighted material:

Catholic University of America Press *(The Fathers of the Church: a New Translation)*
Wm. B. Eerdmans Publishing Co. *(The Ante-Nicene Fathers; the Nicene and Post-Nicene Fathers)*
Paulist Press *(Ancient Christian Writers)*
University of Notre Dame Press *(The Good News and Its Proclamation)*

Note: Translation used is indicated each time by:
  * *New American Bible*
  ** *The Jerusalem Bible*

Scripture texts (*) used in this work are taken from the *New American Bible*, copyright © 1970, by the Confraternity of Christian Doctrine, Washington, D.C., and are used by permission of copyright owner. All rights reserved.

Excerpts (**) from *The Jerusalem Bible*, copyright © 1966, by Darton, Longman & Todd, Ltd. and Doubleday and Company, Inc. Used by permission of the publisher.

Copyright © 1983, by the Daughters of St. Paul

Printed in the U.S.A. by the Daughters of St. Paul
50 St. Paul's Ave., Boston, MA 02130

The Daughters of St. Paul are an international congregation of religious women serving the Church with the communications media.

CONTENTS

Abbreviations for Church Documents and Publications	8
Introduction	9
I. "I Am the Way, the Truth and the Life"	15
Christ the Way	
Christ the Truth	
Christ the Life	
II. "One Is Your Master"	35
Formation of the Mind	
Formation of the Will	
Formation of the Heart	
III. "Anyone Who Loves Me Will Be True to My Word"	57
IV. "I Came from the Father and Have Come into the World"	75
Conclusion	99
Bibliography—Books	105
Bibliography—Documents	109
Prayers for the Catechist	111

Abbreviations for Church Documents and Publications

AA	*Apostolicam actuositatem* Decree on the Apostolate of the Laity
AG	*Ad gentes* Decree on the Missionary Activity of the Church
BT	*Basic Teachings for Catholic Religious Education*
CPG	*Credo of the People of God*
CT	*Catechesi tradendae* On Catechesis in Our Time
DV	*Dei Verbum* Dogmatic Constitution on Divine Revelation
EN	*Evangelii nuntiandi* On Evangelization in the Modern World
GCD	*General Catechetical Directory*
GS	*Gaudium et spes* Pastoral Constitution on the Church in the Modern World
SC	*Sacrosanctum concilium* Constitution on the Sacred Liturgy

Introduction

Before the coming of the Redeemer, the history of mankind clearly shows how far people had strayed from the knowledge and love of the true God. Nevertheless, the Heavenly Father had compassion on mankind and He "spoke in fragmentary and varied ways to our fathers through the prophets..." (Heb. 1:1)* in order to prepare mankind for the coming of the Redeemer who would enlighten them and save them from sin:

> ...in this final age, he has spoken to us through his Son, whom he has made heir of all things and through whom he first created the universe. This Son is the reflection of the Father's glory, the exact representation of the Father's being, and he sustains all things by his powerful word (Heb. 1:2, 3).*

Through His Son, God revealed Himself and His will to mankind.

The revelation of the Father through the Son was carried out by words and deeds "intrinsically bound up with each other" (DV, 2). The deeds performed witnessed to the words; the words proclaimed the deeds and brought to light the mystery they contained (cf. DV, 2).

> The most intimate truth which this revelation gives about God and the salvation of man shines forth in Christ, who is Himself both the mediator and the sum total of Revelation (DV, 2).

So that this revelation should remain in its entirety for the salvation of mankind, Jesus Christ, "in whom the entire Revelation of the most high God is summed up" (DV, 7), commanded His apostles to preach the Gospel, "the source of all saving truth and moral discipline" (DV, 7).

In the Dogmatic Constitution on Divine Revelation, Vatican Council II goes on to aptly express what the Church has always taught regarding the "traditio," the handing on of the deposit of faith:

> What has been handed on by the apostles comprises everything that serves to make the People of God live their lives in holiness and increase their faith. In this way the Church in her doctrine, life and worship, perpetuates and transmits to every generation all that she herself is, all that she believes (DV, 8).

> Sacred Scripture is the speech of God as it is put down in writing under the breath of the Holy Spirit. And Tradition transmits in its entirety the Word of God which has been entrusted to the apostles by Christ the Lord and the Holy Spirit. It transmits it to the successors of the apostles so that, enlightened by the Spirit of truth, they may faithfully preserve, expound, and spread it abroad by their preaching. Thus it comes about that the Church does not draw

her certainty about all revealed truths from the Holy Scripture alone. Hence, both Scripture and Tradition must be accepted and honored with equal feelings of devotion and reverence (DV, 9).

Sacred Tradition and Sacred Scripture make up a single sacred deposit of the Word of God, which is entrusted to the Church.

The task of giving an authentic interpretation of the Word of God, whether in its written form or in the form of Tradition, has been entrusted to the living teaching office of the Church alone. Its authority in this matter is exercised in the name of Jesus Christ. Yet this Magisterium is not superior to the Word of God, but is its servant. It teaches only what has been handed on to it. At the divine command and with the help of the Holy Spirit, it listens to this devotedly, *guards* it with dedication and *expounds* it faithfully. All that it proposes for belief as being divinely revealed is drawn from this SINGLE DEPOSIT OF FAITH.

It is clear, therefore, that, in the supremely wise arrangement of God, Sacred Tradition, Sacred Scripture and the Magisterium of the Church are so connected and associated that one of them cannot stand without the others (DV, 10).

The Church faithfully follows the mandate she received from Jesus Christ, "Go...proclaim the good news...teach..." (cf. Mk. 16:15; Mt. 28:20), because she, like the Heavenly Father:

...wants the whole world to hear the summons to salvation, so that through hearing it may believe, through belief it may hope, through hope it may come to love (DV, 1).

In the Apostolic Exhortation *Catechesi tradendae* of Pope John Paul II, the content of the Church's preaching and teaching is explicit. If catechesis is to be authentic, it must be Christocentric.

> ...at the heart of catechesis we find, in essence, a Person, the Person of Jesus of Nazareth, "the only Son from the Father...full of grace and truth," who suffered and died for us and who now, after rising, is living with us forever. It is Jesus who is "the way, and the truth, and the life," and Christian living consists in following Christ....
>
> The primary and essential object of catechesis is "the mystery of Christ." Catechizing is in a way to lead a person to study this mystery in all its dimensions (CT, 5).
>
> Christocentricity in catechesis also means the intention to transmit not one's own teaching or that of some other master, but the teaching of Jesus Christ, the Truth that He communicates or, to put it more precisely, the Truth that He is (CT, 6).
>
> Authentic catechesis is always an orderly and systematic initiation into the revelation that God has given of Himself to humanity in Christ Jesus, a revelation stored in the depths of the Church's memory and in Sacred Scripture, and constantly communicated from one generation to the next by a living, active *traditio* (CT, 22).

The purpose of this study is to examine the spirituality centered on Jesus, the Way, and the Truth, and the Life, as applied to catechetics, and to determine that it has the potential to resolve imbalances in catechetical methodology. The Way, Truth and Life spirituality as set forth by Reverend James Alberione has this possibility, because by its very nature it leads the whole person to the whole Christ.

The writer intends to examine the nature of the Way, Truth and Life spirituality through the study of selected writings of Reverend James Alberione (1884-1971), Founder of the Pauline Congregations.

Then, recourse will be had to Church sources and documents, including selected writings from the Fathers of the Church, to establish the fact that the roots of the Way, Truth and Life method are evangelical and ecclesial.

By its very nature, the Way, Truth and Life method is Christocentric and fulfills the directive of the *General Catechetical Directory*, which states: "Catechesis must necessarily be Christocentric" (GCD, 40).

When implemented correctly, the Way, Truth and Life method can bring the student to a deeper knowledge of the Person of Jesus Christ, Who is the central fact of Revelation and the "heart of catechesis" (CT, 5). The very purpose of the method is to form the whole person—mind, will and heart (sentiments)—in Christ.

A catechist who studies the Way, Truth and Life spirituality and puts it into practice in his/her own life will, as a result, not transmit his/her own teaching, but will communicate the teaching of Christ Himself, which comes through the Magisterium of the Church.

The catechist, then, by means of instruction and example, will be able to help his/her students meet the challenges that adult life presents in our day. Students will be convinced of their Faith and will live by their convictions—formed by the teachings of the Church.

Founded by Father James Alberione, the Daughters of St. Paul have the specific mission of evangelization through the media of social communication, and as a directive of their Founder states: "Catechetics must have a prime place in our mission."

In researching the writings of Father Alberione, this writer hopes to reach a deeper understanding and appreciation of his charism, his zeal, and the ideal that spurred him to accomplish so much in his lifetime. His ardent desire was that Jesus Christ, the Way, Truth and Life, be lived by his sons and daughters—"Christ lives in me"—and be preached to all; that the doctrine of the Divine Master reach the very ends of the earth: with the Church, in the Church, and from the Church.

I. "I Am the Way, the Truth and the Life" (Jn. 14:6)*

The Gospel account of St. John records the last discourse of Jesus, wherein He presents a self-definition:

> "Do not let your hearts be troubled.
> Have faith in God
> and faith in me.
> In my Father's house there are many dwelling places;
> otherwise, how could I have told you
> that I was going to prepare a place for you?
> I am indeed going to prepare a place for you,
> and then I shall come back to take you with me,
> that where I am you also may be.
> You know the way that leads where I go."

"Lord," said Thomas, "we do not know where you are going. How can we know the way?" Jesus told him:

> "I am the way, and the truth, and the life;
> no one comes to the Father but through me.

> If you really knew me, you would know my Father also.
>
> From this point on you know him: you have seen him."
>
> "Lord," Philip said to him, "show us the Father and that will be enough for us." "Philip," Jesus replied, "after I have been with you all this time, you still do not know me?
>
> "Whoever has seen me has seen the Father" (Jn. 14:1-9).*

Christ's own words: "I am the way, and the truth, and the life" introduce a basic Christological doctrine related to the education and the formation of the whole person in the whole Christ.

Jesus gave various descriptions of Himself:

> "I am the light of the world."
> "I am the vine."
> "I am the good shepherd."

But these are particular aspects of Jesus. When He wanted to describe Himself completely, He said: "I am the way, and the truth, and the life."[1]

Inspired by the encyclical of Leo XIII *Tametsi futura* (Nov. 1, 1900), the seminarian James Alberione began to penetrate more deeply the mystery of Christ. Through the reading of the Gospel, the future founder of the Pauline Congregations viewed Christ as the Master, the Teacher Who forms the whole person: mind, will and heart. The encyclical of Leo XIII which outlined the meaning of "way, truth and life," together with the concept of Christ the Master, contains the seed of Father Alberione's practical and dynamic Christology. He, therefore, placed the Divine Master, Way, Truth and Life as the center of the spirituality of his Pauline religious family, and as the main content of their mission of evangelization.

The brief writings of Father Alberione on the birth of the Pauline Family reflect the influence that *Tametsi futura* had on him as a young seminarian. Using the third person singular, Father Alberione describes his thoughts and prayers during his adoration vigil between December 31, 1900, and January 1, 1901:

> The night which divided the last century from the present one was decisive for the specific mission and particular spirit in which the Pauline Family was to be born and to live.
>
> He had read Pope Leo XIII's invitation to pray for the century that was about to begin.
>
> A special light came from the Host, a greater understanding of the invitation extended by Jesus: "Come to me, all of you..." (Mt. 11:28). He seemed to understand the heart of the great Pope, the calls sent out by the Church, the true mission of the priest.... He felt deeply obliged to prepare himself to do something for God and the men of the new century with whom he would live.
>
> As he thought about the future, it seemed to him that in the new century generous souls would feel what he had felt....
>
> He prayed that the new century might be born in the Eucharistic Christ, that new apostles would reform laws, schools, literature. the press, customs; that the Church would launch a new mission campaign, that the new means of apostolate would

> be used well, that society would accept the great teachings of Pope Leo XIII's encyclicals.
>
> The Eucharist, the Gospel, the Pope, the new century...
>
> From then on, these thoughts were to guide his reading, studies, prayer and entire formation. Though at first the idea was very confused, with the passing of the years it grew clearer and then became concrete.
>
> He remained with the basic thought that it is necessary to develop the entire human personality: mind, heart, and will, for one's own salvation and for a more fruitful apostolate.[2]

Fifty-six years after his initial inspiration and forty-two years after the actual foundation of the Society of St. Paul, the impact of the encyclical was still evident.

To his spiritual sons, Father Alberione wrote:

> "The common good requires that we have recourse to Jesus Christ, Way, Truth and Life" (Leo XIII, Encyclical Letter, *Tametsi futura*).
>
> The Pope says that genuine piety manifested during the Holy Year offers good promise for the new century. It is a piety directed to Jesus Christ, Way, Truth and Life....
>
> The more we become part of Him, the more we will live in spiritual health. Living Christ integrally the whole man will be sound—sound in mind, heart, will and body, morally sound. "We have been given a pledge of future glory."[3]

All of the writings, letters, sermons, conferences, and exhortations of Father Alberione to his spiritual sons and daughters were directed to one purpose: "I don't have silver or gold, but I give you what I do have: Jesus Christ, Way, Truth and Life."[4]

Christ the Way

Sin disfigured the image of God in man, by sowing the spirit of rebellion in his will, diffusing ignorance and error in his intellect and stirring evil passions in his heart.

As a consequence of sin, man sought happiness in creatures instead of tending toward his Creator, for Whom he was made. The result was a never-ending restlessness of spirit.

Redemption was necessary in order to restore the image of God in man.

Jesus came into the world to raise up man from his fallen state and place him on the level destined for him by the Father. To do this Christ chose to become like us in all things but sin (cf. Heb. 4:15). He was the first to walk the way that would lead us back to the Father. He atoned for our sins by dying on the cross. Thus He made us partakers of the divine life, which makes us children of God. Jesus made us sons of God and made Himself our way to the Father because He is our Mediator, our Brother. "No one comes to the Father but through me" (Jn. 14:6).*[5]

As the Way, Jesus guides the will of man toward eternal goods and reunites him to the Father according to the divine plan of our predestination.

> God chose us in him before the world began, to be holy and blameless in his sight, to be full of love; he likewise predestined us through Christ Jesus to be his adopted sons—such was his will and pleasure—that all might praise the glorious favor he has bestowed on us in his beloved. It is in Christ and through his blood that we have been redeemed and our sins forgiven, so immeasurably generous is God's favor to us (Eph. 1:4-8).*

To the rich young man who asked the question, "Master, what shall I do to gain eternal life?" Jesus answered, "...if you will enter into life, keep the commandments..." (cf. Mt. 19:16-22).

The imperative is here. Eternal life hinges on obedience to God's law. We must then follow His doctrine not just when He teaches virtue, but more especially when He practices it. Jesus well knew human nature and He knows that men learn more from example than from word. When we look at Jesus' life, we see the most perfect harmony between what He taught and what He did.

Jesus preached humility, but first He gave the example: "Learn from me for I am gentle and humble of heart" (Mt. 11:29).* St. Paul tells us that Jesus "humbled himself, obediently accepting even death, death on a cross" (Phil. 2:8).* He taught charity, love of God above all things, and love of neighbor as oneself. In the sacrifice of Calvary He gave the greatest proof of His love for God and for mankind.

Father Alberione comments:

> Many have wanted to reform the Church, but without reforming themselves first. They possessed neither a mission nor virtue nor true piety. Jesus

Christ, however, first set the example Himself, preached His doctrine, and died to win grace for us.[6]

Imitation proves love—a love that consists not in words or feelings alone, but in *doing* what the Lord asks of us.

> In the Christian religion the first and most necessary condition is docility to the precepts of Jesus Christ.... (And) the law of Christ must be sought in the Church. Christ is man's "Way"; the Church also is his "Way"—Christ of Himself and by His very nature, the Church by His commission and the communication of His power.... He willed to perpetuate the office assigned to Him by His Father by means of the ministry of the Church.[7]

Father Alberione echoes the thought of Leo XIII:

> In this Church we are not called to live on the branches, but to be branches and to produce abundant fruits (cf. Jn. 15:16).[8]

> Nothing is more salutary and profitable than making ourselves devoted children and docile disciples of this divine Church, to learn all she teaches, to let ourselves be guided by her and to accept all the means of sanctification.[9]

Father Timothy Giaccardo, Servant of God, and spiritual son of Father Alberione of the "first hour," summarizes the Pauline understanding of Jesus as Way:

> The Divine Master is the Way: not only because He pointed out to man the way that leads to heaven and reunites man with the Father, and not only because by His example He made Himself our model. Jesus Master is the Way because only in Him and through Him can man reach the Father. He not

only precedes as a model to imitate; rather He carries man with Himself and in Himself as the body carries its members.[10]

Christ the Truth

Jesus, Who is the personal, uncreated, eternal Wisdom of the Father, knows the Father perfectly and so can express the Father perfectly. While He is Wisdom, He is also the Word through Whom the Father expresses Himself, His nature, and His perfections. Through the Word, the Father expresses Himself in a living and real image[11]: "The Word became flesh and made his dwelling among us" (Jn. 1:14),* perfectly equal to the Father: "...and the Word was God" (Jn. 1:1).* Jesus' teachings and His work are always, then, the revelation of the Father: "The Father is in me and I in him" (Jn. 10:38).* "Whoever has seen me has seen the Father" (Jn. 14:9).* We can know the Father, therefore, only through the revelation of Jesus, the Son. More expressly: as a condition for knowing God, Who is Truth,[12] it is necessary to hear and accept the word of Christ, Who said: "I am the Truth" (cf. Jn. 14:6).

Leo XIII states:

> Wherefore if the Truth be sought by the human intellect, it must first of all submit itself to Jesus Christ and securely rest upon His teaching, since therein Truth itself speaks.[13]

Father Alberione expresses himself in a similar way:

> However many ideologies have arisen or are about to arise, we must always confront them with

the doctrine of Jesus Christ and *accept them only if they are in conformity with it*. No matter how much time passes or studies progress, Jesus always remains the only infallible Teacher whose doctrine is eminent, certain and indestructible.[14]

Because Jesus gave us the truths that form the object of our faith—from the truth regarding the essence of the One and Triune God, to the truth regarding our eternal destiny and our sharing in the happiness of God, we should humbly listen to His word in Sacred Scripture and more especially in the Gospel. We should listen to His word as it comes to us through the teachings of the Church.

> God...holds supreme dominion over man's intellect as well as over his will. By obeying Christ with his intellect man by no means acts in a servile manner, but in complete accordance with his reason and his natural dignity For by his will he yields nor to the authority of any man, but to that of God, the Author of his being, and the first principle to whom he is subject by the very law of his nature. He does not suffer himself to be forced only by the theories of any human teacher, but by the eternal and unchangeable truth.[15]

As the God-man, Jesus brought His truth and His grace to mankind. His truth shows us the way that leads to our goal His grace strengthens us so that we can achieve our goal. Through the work of the Holy Spirit, Jesus communicates the gifts of His Wisdom:

> When the Spirit of truth comes he will lead you to the complete truth, since he will not be speaking

as from himself, but will say only what he has learned; ...all he tells you will be taken from what is mine (Jn. 16:13-14).*

"The gifts which concern the intellect," states Father Alberione, "complete the work of the Divine Master in the person."

—Through the gift of *wisdom,* in fact, we acquire not only a theoretical knowledge of things but also an experiential knowledge, and we can enjoy and savor the truth. When the Spirit infuses this gift in us, the soul is filled with joy and happiness in the contemplation of eternal truths;
—with the gift of *knowledge* He helps us know things in their real meaning: what we are, who God is, our strong points and our weaknesses;
—with the gift of *understanding* He helps us know the divine truths with more depth.[16]

A synthesis of Father Alberione's thought regarding Jesus Truth is found in this brief statement of Father Timothy Giaccardo:

Jesus Master is the Truth not only because He preached and taught eternal truths or because He communicated to men the understanding of these truths. Jesus is the Truth because He makes us know, believe and live "all that He has learned from the Father."[17]

Christ the Life

After the fall of our first parents, God promised a redeemer (Gn. 3:15), and the prophets of Israel kept this thought continually before the people. For centuries the people looked forward to the coming of the Messiah. With the passing of time, however, the true concept of the redeemer faded. Years of oppression under powerful invaders and misinterpretation of prophecies led the Israelite people to imagine the Messiah as an earthly conqueror who would free his people from the yoke of oppression.

When the Messiah did enter the history of Israel, he was not a mere man. He was the God-man, Jesus Christ, Who is the Second Person of the Trinity. He, the Son of God, took to Himself a human nature to release man from the punishment of original sin and regain for him divine grace—*supernatural life.*

Only a man who is also God was able to offer just reparation for man's offense against God. Because Jesus is God, all of His actions and prayers had an infinite value. The sufferings of His passion and death gained for us new life, that is, forgiveness of sin (cf. Eph. 2:1-7), and sanctifying grace, which is the *supernatural life of the soul* (cf. Jn. 1:16). "I came that they might have life and have it to the full" (cf. Jn 10:10).

We can say with certainty, then, that by dying on the cross for us, Jesus became our life.

Leo XIII states that Christ is Life because He merited eternal life for us, and because He is Life by His very nature:

> God alone is Life. All other beings partake of life, but *are* not life. Christ from all eternity and by His very nature is "the Life," just as He is the Truth,

because He is God of God. From Him, as from its most sacred source, all life pervades and ever will pervade creation. Whatever is, is by Him; whatever lives, lives by Him. For by the Word "all things were made; and without him was made nothing that was made." This is true of the natural life; but...we have a much higher and better life, won for us by Christ's mercy, that is to say, "the life of grace," whose happy consummation is "the life of glory," to which all our thoughts and actions ought to be directed.[18]

Father Alberione uses the Gospel of John as the basis for his consideration regarding Jesus-Life:

"In him was life, and the life was the light of men" (Jn. 1:4). And this life of light and of grace makes us children of God: "To as many as received him he gave the power of becoming sons of God" (Jn. 1:12). He draws life from the Father and communicates it to us: "Of his fullness we have all received, grace for grace" (Jn. 1:16). He is the vine which bears the branches and communicates life to them. We are the branches. Apart from Him there is only desolation, death, sin, and damnation.

Jesus wants to be our life: "I came that they may have life, and have it more abundantly" (Jn. 10:10). It is the Father's will, too, that we receive life from Jesus: "In this is my Father glorified, that you may bear very much fruit, and become my disciples" (Jn. 15:8).[19]

The supernatural life that Jesus merited for us, He communicates to us especially by means of the sacraments. Father Alberione emphasizes the Eucharist as "the true font of grace, in which we receive the very Author of grace."[20]

It is in Communion that our natural life is replaced by the divine life of Jesus Christ. Grafted into Jesus we will produce supernatural fruits. We will speak and think as Jesus; live of Jesus; die with Jesus. We will have no other ideal than to be a living image of Jesus Christ: "I live now not with my own life but with the life of Christ who lives in me" (Gal. 2:20).[21]

The Eucharistic Jesus was always the source and center of Father Alberione's apostolic activities. The specific form of prayer that he strongly recommended to the Pauline Family was the daily Hour of Adoration before the Blessed Sacrament. He saw this hour as a time for learning. The Teacher? Jesus the Divine Master, Way, Truth and Life.

> His work of teaching does not limit itself to the ear, but penetrates within. He created our mind, our will, our heart, and He enlightens us, because *He is the light* which gives light to every man who comes into this world (cf. Jn. 1:9).
>
> Perhaps we have rarely given consideration to the profound meaning of this expression: the Word is the light and the *light is the life* (cf. Jn. 1:4).[22]

Father Timothy Giaccardo, faithful interpreter of Father Alberione's thought, concludes:

> Jesus Master is Life not only because He merited grace for us through His prayer and suffering, and not only because He communicates through the sacraments the grace that penetrates, empowers, restores and elevates the whole human person. Jesus is Life because He is present and active in us. In Him and through Him we live in God. We are His heirs and have the promise of eternal life.[23]

As an intimate follower of St. Paul, Father Alberione had a completely Christ-centered thought. In the writings of St. Paul he found the most profound interpretation of the Christian mystery. In the Apostle's understanding of Jesus Master, Way, Truth and Life, Father Alberione found the most complete structural synthesis of Christianity.

Although St. Paul never referred to Jesus as Way, Truth and Life, Father Alberione finds the basis for his Christological thought in Paul's interpretation of the unity of all things in Christ.

> God has given us the wisdom to understand fully the mystery, the plan he was pleased to decree in Christ, to be carried out in the fullness of time: namely, to bring all things in the heavens and on earth into one under Christ's headship (Eph. 1:7-10).*

This unity or synthesis includes the whole person, elevates all of his faculties and human activities, perfecting them with supernatural gifts.

Christ is one. After naming Himself in various ways for our understanding (Shepherd, Door, Messiah, Light, etc.), He gave the all-inclusive and complete self-definition: "I am the Way, Truth and Life."

Christ taught men how to follow Him, how to conform their lives to His teachings and resemble Him in their mind, will and heart (sentiments). Christ will live in man without lessening his freedom; instead He will elevate it. Man will still have his human personality, but the divine person of Christ will make him a new "divine" being modeled on the divine form of Christ Himself.[24]

As a result of this transformation of mankind, all things natural and supernatural, in the heavens and on the earth, will be brought into one under Christ's headship.

This process of transformation or Christification, as Father Alberione has called it, begins with Christian formation, and the formation of the Christian is accomplished through systematic catechesis.

THE DEVOTION TO JESUS MASTER, WAY, TRUTH AND LIFE IS THE COMPLETE PRESENTATION OF THE CHRISTIAN MYSTERY

In Jesus Master, Way, Truth and Life is the most organic and complete synthesis of Christianity.

GOD
One and Triune

FATHER	SON	HOLY SPIRIT
Supreme Good	Eternal Truth	Infinite Love

MAN
One person, triune in activity

Will	*Mind*	*Heart (Sentiments)*
Tends toward the good	Tends toward the truth	Tends to love
To serve God	To know God	To love God

REDEMPTION
accomplished by
JESUS CHRIST

Who Is:

The Way	*The Truth*	*The Life*
King and Shepherd	Prophet and Teacher	Priest and Victim
Brings the will of man back to the desire for heavenly goods—to the Heavenly Father.	Elevates the mind of man to the mysteries of God and to eternal truths.	Restores charity to man's heart, which is divine life.

Christian Life Is the Exercise of:

Hope	*Faith*	*Charity*
Union with God the font of all happiness	Union with God the font of truth	Union with God Who is Love

THE CHURCH

Christ lives in His Church which is One yet Triune in its modes of Activity

Way	*Truth*	*Life*
Law (Code)	Teachings (Creed)	Sacraments (Cult)

The Church is nourished by

THE EUCHARIST

Memorial of His Passion	Mystery of Faith	Sacred Banquet

"Pledge of Future Glory"

ETERNAL LIFE IS:

The possession of God the Supreme Good	The vision of God Who is Eternal Truth	The love of God Who is Infinite Love

FOOTNOTES—CHAPTER ONE

1. James Alberione, S.S.P., S.T.D., "Jesus Master and Christian Formation," *Pauline Spirituality* (Boston: Daughters of St. Paul, 1974), p. 171.
2. Alberione, *"Abundantes Divitiae Gratiae Suae"* (Boston: Daughters of St. Paul, 1979), pp. 14-17.
3. Alberione, *Carissimi in San Paolo*, ed. Rosario F. Esposito (Rome: Edizioni Paoline, 1971), p. 1224.
4. Ibid., p. 63.
5. Cf. Alberione, "Practical Devotion to Jesus Master, Way, Truth and Life," *Pauline Spirituality*, p. 334.
6. Alberione, *Ut Perfectus Sit Homo Dei*, vol. I (Rome: Edizioni Paoline, 1960-62), p. 516.
7. Pope Leo XIII, *Tametsi futura prospicientibus* (Boston: St. Paul Editions, 1979), pp. 13, 14.
8. Alberione, *Prediche del Primo Maestro* (Rome: Figlie di San Paolo, 1954), pp. 45-50.
9. Alberione, *Meditation on Christian Formation*, Haec Meditare, Serie Prima, vol. IV (Rome: Figlie di San Paolo, 1948-1949).
10. Timothy Giaccardo, S.S.P., *Dai Tetti in Su* (Rome: Edizioni Paoline, 1956), p. 6.
11. Cf. Alberione, *Gesù Maestro*, Haec Meditare, Serie Prima, vol. III.
12. What is true *is*. What is not true is *not*. By self-definition, God IS (Ex. 3:14) and is, therefore, Truth.
13. Leo XIII, *Tametsi futura prospicientibus*, p. 15.
14. Alberione, *Meditation on Christian Formation*, Haec Meditare, Serie Prima, vol. IV.

15. Leo XIII, *Tametsi futura prospicientibus*, p. 16.
16. Alberione, *Gesu Maestro*, Haec Meditare, Serie Prima, vol. III.
17. Giaccardo, *Dai Tetti in Su*, p. 7.
18. Leo XIII, *Tametsi futura prospicientibus*, pp. 17-18.
19. Alberione, "Devotion to Jesus Master, Way, Truth and Life," *Pauline Spirituality*, pp. 336-337.
20. Ibid., p. 293.
21. Alberione, Meditation to the community of Rome, 1948.
22. Alberione, *Gesù Maestro*, Haec Meditare, Serie Prima, vol. III.
23. Giaccardo, *Dai Tetti in Su*, p. 8.
24. Cf. Alberione, Introduction to *Maestro, Via, Verità e Vita*, vol. I, by C. T. Dragone, S.S.P. (Rome: Edizioni Paoline, 1961).

II. "One Is Your Master"
(cf. Mt. 23:8)

In the Gospels Jesus is addressed as "Rabbi" or "Teacher"[1] more often than by any other title. His disciples and even His adversaries addressed Him as such and Jesus acknowledged the title:

> You address me as "Teacher" and "Lord,"
> and fittingly enough,
> for that is what I am (Jn. 13:13).*

Before Pilate He affirmed His mission:

> The reason I was born,
> the reason why I came into the world,
> is to testify to the truth (Jn. 18:37).*

And the crowds recognized the fact that He did not teach as the others did. He taught with authority. "The people were spellbound by his teaching because he taught with authority, and not like the scribes" (Mk. 1:22).*

The Gospels, then, present Jesus as Master or Teacher. Certainly the words of Jesus had an immediate significance for His listeners at that time, but they also have a value that transcends time and locale. In our day the words of Jesus should be even more significant: "Only one is your teacher, the Messiah" (Mt. 23:8).*

From the earliest writings of Father Alberione, it is evident that his concept of the Jesus of the Gospel was that of Jesus Master. To this title he linked the trinomial Way, Truth and Life, and it was in this spirituality that he formed the members of the Pauline Family. Jesus Master, Way, Truth and Life, is the total Christ, and only in Him is the total person formed.

> The full and comprehensive concept of Master as it relates to every man and all of humanity, regarding both human and supernatural elevation, is incarnated in Christ: "I am the way, truth and life" (Jn. 14:6). St. Leo the Great wrote, "In vain will we call ourselves Christians if we do not conform ourselves to Jesus Christ, who declared Himself the Way, so that the life of the Master will become a model for the disciple."
>
> This conformity to Jesus Christ involves the whole man: intellect, sentiment and will.[2]

Jesus is the one true Master sent by the Father:

> After he was baptized by John in the Jordan, Jesus came out of the water, the heavens opened, and the Spirit of God descended upon him as a dove. And behold a voice from the sky said: "This is my Son, the Beloved; he enjoys my favor. Listen to him" (Mt. 17:5).*[3]

With these words of the Father, Jesus was constituted Master, and upon us was imposed the obligation to listen to Him.

Jesus is Teacher or Master because He is the Truth that enlightens every man who comes into the world (cf. Jn. 1:9). He communicates eternal, supernatural truths to man, as well as the grace to believe.

Jesus is the Master because He is the Way that leads to the Father. He traced out for man the sure way to reach the Father: "You have heard it said...but I say to you..." (cf. Mt. 5:21, 27, 33). Speaking thus, He communicates the grace of hope.

Finally, Jesus is the Master because He is also the Life. He gives man sanctifying grace—a sharing in God's own life, as well as the grace to understand His teachings and put them into practice. By so doing, man conforms his life to that of the Master and lives the fullness of human life and also supernatural life.

Jesus Master, Way, Truth and Life, living and active in the Eucharist and in the Church, is the total Christ. A knowledge of the mystery of Christ in the light of Jesus Master, Way, Truth and Life, will influence the education and formation of the Christian—the formation of the total person. To each person, Jesus Master offers light for the mind through the study of His doctrine. He offers a sure way for the will in its journey to the Father through the practice of the Commandments, the virtues, the works of mercy. He offers supernatural life through the grace which flows from the sacraments administered by His Church.

Salvation is in Jesus Master, not only eternal salvation but also the salvation of human values.

With the purpose in view of forming the total person, Father Alberione writes:

> We must form the person who is wise, just, sociable and upright before God, himself and society.
>
> Then we can form the Christian who follows Jesus Christ, Way, Truth and Life—through living faith, imitation of the Master, life in Christ and in the Church.[4]

As a seminarian, Father Alberione was a catechist for six years. He studied pedagogy under the Brothers of the Christian Schools; then, from 1910 to 1914, he studied catechetical methods and catechetical organization in parishes, as well as the spiritual, intellectual and pedagogical formation of catechists.

For three years he did catechetical work in the boys' oratory and taught religion to public school students.[5]

Later he wrote:

> All of these stages were disposed by a gentle and loving Providence....
>
> Acts of the Holy See regarding catechetics, good catechetical texts, work for the formation of catechists, catechetical films and filmstrips, posters, catechetical equipment—all served in the hands of God.[6]

When the bishop appointed Father Alberione to the Diocesan Catechetical Commission which established texts and diocesan catechetical programs, he made a special study and apostolate of catechetics: Catechetics was always regarded as the first and fundamental undertaking: "Go, preach, teach" (cf. Mt. 28:19; Mk. 16:15).[7]

Father Alberione viewed the formation of a Christian as the formation of "another Christ"—namely, a complete formation or education linked to instruction. The total person is formed in the total Christ—Way, Truth and Life.

In addressing the group attending the first Pauline Catechetical Convention, he stressed that the Way, Truth and Life method of Christian formation is not reserved to the Pauline Congregations. Jesus taught this same method with His life. True Christian formation must be directed to the total person:

> Our method is not only "ours," because it is not a reserved method, but it is *the* method which the Lord taught with His life. We must bring the whole man to God. We cannot make him Christian only in mind, or Christian only in sentiments, or Christian only in prayer or in works.
>
> It is necessary that man live Jesus Christ with his entire being and in his entire being, because Christ is the unique way to go to the Father....
>
> We must make the entire man Christian. We cannot make only one part grow.... Every fractionalization leads to deviation.[8]

Moreover, Father Alberione regarded Christian formation as it is "understood by the Church and set forth in Pius XI's encyclical, *Divini illius Magistri*":[9]

> ...Christian education embraces the whole extension of human life: physical and spiritual, intel-

> lectual and moral life, individual, domestic and social, not with a view of reducing it in any way, but in order to elevate, regulate and perfect it according to the examples and teaching of Christ....
>
> It should never be forgotten that the subject of Christian education concerns man as a whole, soul united to body by nature, together with all his faculties, natural and supernatural....
>
> There can be no true education which is not Christian education.[10]

The following statement of Father Alberione echoes the thought of Pius XI and, at the same time, provides the basis for our study of catechetics in the light of the Way, Truth and Life method.

> Religion in its totality is dogma, morality and liturgy. These three aspects are fused because man is one.... In Him all the faculties are integrated....[11]
>
> For this reason, communicate the truth...and make it be lived. Education is the moral aspect of teaching.[12]

The decree *Christus Dominus* renews these same facts while relating them to catechetical instruction. "Its function," the decree explains, "is to develop in men a living, explicit and active faith, enlightened by doctrine" (CD, 14).

In his Apostolic Exhortation *Catechesi tradendae*, His Holiness Pope John Paul II reiterates the mind of the Church in defining catechesis as:

> ...an education of children, young people and adults in the faith, which includes especially the teaching of Christian doctrine imparted...in an or-

ganic and systematic way, with a view to initiating the hearers into the fullness of Christian life (CT, 18).

In the light of Way, Truth and Life, catechesis is doctrine applied to practical living and expressed through worship. The mind, the will and the heart are formed in Christ. As TRUTH, Jesus directs the intellect to eternal truths which alone can answer all the questions of the human soul. As WAY, He guides the will of man to eternal goods and reconciliation with the Father. As LIFE, Jesus restores charity in the heart through grace.

Formation of the Mind

The first of man's faculties to be formed through catechesis is the mind, because the mind influences and determines the action of the will. It is the mind or intellect that should direct one's life. Catechesis "cannot neglect the formation of a religious way of thinking" (GCD, 88). Ideas that are formed in the mind are principles of action. Man lives his daily life according to the ideas he has formed. These ideas become convictions. Father Alberione writes:

> From our thoughts come our words, sentiments, and actions. It is the mind that guides us, as a pilot at the controls of his plane or a driver at the wheel of his car.[13]

Authentic catechesis forms the mind by presenting the truths of faith, morals and worship concretely, adopting them to the intellectual level of the learner.[14]

Christianity is not a synthesis of abstract formulas; it is a way of life lived in a personal relationship with the Trinity. Jesus Master Himself pointed out that doctrine should become a part of daily life: "Man does not live on bread alone but on every word that comes from the mouth of God" (Mt. 4:4).**

The aim of catechesis is to bring the Christian to a deeper understanding of the mystery of Christ in the light of God's word, to a knowledge of the kingdom of God that He announced, to a knowledge and understanding of the requirements and promises contained in His Gospel message and in the demands He set down for anyone wanting to follow Him.[15] This understanding, this knowledge, is acquired through systematic instruction and study of the truths contained in the Creed, the deposit of faith, entrusted to the Church by Christ Himself.

Instruction in "the faith which we believe" must lead to a deepening of "the faith by which we believe," that is, the theological virtue of faith infused in the soul by God at Baptism. By the virtue of faith the intellect rests in God, because the knowledge that comes from Revelation is more secure, more perfect than the knowledge which comes from the intellect or the senses. "Faith rests not on the wisdom of men but on the power of God" (1 Cor. 2:5).* As the basis of Christian morality, faith must show itself in deeds. "It is not those who say to me, 'Lord, Lord,' who will enter the kingdom of heaven, but the person who does the will of my Father in heaven" (Mt. 7:21).* Above all, faith must show itself in love of God and love of neighbor. "On these two commandments the whole law is based, and the prophets as well" (Mt. 22:40).*

Father Alberione writes:

> Intelligence and deep faith lead to clear knowledge of the end and means. "Nothing is willed which is not first known." Profound convictions, abundant instruction, and the spirit of faith are necessary to move the will efficaciously. All this influences the will, producing resoluteness, firmness, constancy.[6]

Formation of the Will

The will, the governing faculty of man, and the intellect were created by God to work together in harmony. The function of the intellect is to seek the truth; that of the will is to embrace the good. Generally speaking, the intellect directs the will because one cannot desire or reject what he does not know.

The will does not exercise an absolute power over the sense faculties, but rather a kind of moral influence or power of persuasion that leads these lower faculties to obedience.

The freedom that man exercises through his will is not absolute but relative. This means that the will does not have a "right" to choose evil. Its legitimate freedom consists in its power to choose between two or more good objects, or between options that the intellect has proposed and which are in conformity with the truth.

Vatican II explains that the very dignity of man lies in his right use of freedom:

> Man's dignity requires him to act out of conscious and free choice, as moved and drawn in

a personal way from within, and not by blind impulses in himself or by mere external constraint. Man gains such dignity when, ridding himself of all slavery to the passions, he presses forward towards his goal by freely choosing what is good, and, by his diligence and skill, effectively secures for himself the means suited to this end. Since human freedom has been weakened by sin it is only by the help of God's grace that man can give his actions their full and proper relationship to God. Before the judgment seat of God an account of his own life will be rendered to each one according as he has done either good or evil (GS, 17).

The will is free, and it gives this freedom to its own acts and to the acts of the other faculties that it influences. Consequently, it confers merit or demerit on these same actions.

Father Alberione writes: "To regulate the will means to regulate the whole person."[17]

The privilege of catechesis is to form the will of the Christian.

Although potentially our strongest faculty, the will is a delicate instrument that needs guidance and discipline. With the help of God's grace it is always possible for the will to exercise control, provided its freedom is not temporarily affected by some passion—for example, a very strong impulse of anger. With effort, the sense faculties and passions are brought under the influence of the will. To strengthen the will it is necessary to continue making the right choices no matter what difficulty arises. Time by time, whether easy or hard, the right choice is to be made.

To make the right choices one must be impelled by knowledge of God and love for Him. The will operates out of love, so the stronger one's love for the Highest Good, God, the stronger will be one's motive for making those choices which lead him to gain more of God's love.

Spiritual formation of the will cannot take place apart from the mind. It must be stimulated by faith arising from a supernaturally enlightened intellect.

Proper formation of the will, states Father Alberione, requires "firmness, skill and grace, and first of all, great light, conviction and faith."[18]

Convictions guide and stimulate the will. The Divine Master Himself stressed the necessity of applying to daily life the truths He taught: "Anyone who hears my words and puts them into practice is like the wise man who built his house on rock" (Mt. 7:24).* Jesus' aim was to influence the behavior of His listeners, but He always presented His moral teachings as the fullness of life in true freedom. Happiness was promised to those who put His teachings into practice: "Blest are they who hear the word of God and keep it" (Lk. 11:28) * Although the Master's teachings were always presented from a positive point of view, they carried with them an imperative:

> "The Son of Man will come with his Father's glory accompanied by his angels. When he does, he will repay each man according to his conduct" (Mt. 16:27).*

Catechesis, therefore, must include not only those things which are to be believed, but also those things which are to be done (GCD, 63).

Catechesis forms the will by positive means: first through the convictions which have been established through instruction in the truths of faith. These convictions will be both guide and stimulus to the will. Then, catechesis presents models for imitation—Christ, the Blessed Mother, the saints. Instruction appeals to the intellect, but example stimulates the will. Moral ideals become attractive when they are exemplified in a living person.

Father Alberione stresses this point:

> To learn from the examples of Jesus and to imitate His virtues is not left to our freedom. As a Christian, it is an obligation.[19]

The *General Catechetical Directory* exhorts:

> ...active pedagogy should not be satisfied with external expressions only, however useful they may be, but it should strive to bring forth a response from the heart and a taste for prayer (GCD, 79).

With prayer comes an increase of the theological virtue of hope, which implants itself in the will not simply as passive expectation, but rather as a means to move and coordinate spiritual energies. The will desires the reward promised and trusts that God will give the natural and supernatural helps necessary for keeping His Commandments.

> We know that affliction makes for endurance, and endurance for tested virtue, and tested virtue for hope. And this hope will not leave us disappointed (Rom. 5:3-5).*

Formation of the Heart

Man acts as man primarily by exerting the power of his intellect and his will. However, the cognitive powers and the volitional powers of man do not constitute the total person. If catechesis is to form the whole person in Christ, its efforts must also be directed to man's affective powers, that is, the sentiments of his heart.

Emotions, or feelings that arise in a person because of the awareness of something that is pleasing or displeasing to him, were intended by the Creator to be controlled by the intellect and will.

Antiquity has placed the seat of man's affective life in the heart, probably because emotions (e.g., anger, fear, joy, sadness) are accompanied by certain bodily reactions. Later discoveries modified this ancient theory: however, the symbolism has remained. And so, the emotions are to the affective state of man what the heart is to the physical make-up of man. The heart is not the brain, nor is it the blood, but without the heart, the blood does not flow and the brain does not function.

For centuries, the emotions, the sentiments, the passions of man, have been the object of study and observation, yet Sacred Scripture states the most significant conclusion:

> More torturous than all else is the human heart, beyond remedy, who can understand it? (Jer. 17:9)*

For you know every heart—you alone know the hearts of all mankind (1 Kgs. 8:39).**

Everything God created is good (cf. Gn. 1), but, due to the consequences of original sin, man's original integrity was disrupted (cf. Gn. 3). Passions,[20] then, are neither morally good nor morally bad. They become one or the other when the will accepts them, thereby making them voluntary. When the will permits a disorder in the passions, they are evil. Passions that are controlled by reason (i.e., the will enlightened by the intellect), can be occasions of virtue.

Following the thought of St. Thomas, Father Alberione writes:

> From the heart's center proceed the passions. Those of the concupiscible appetite are: love, hate, desire, aversion, joy and sadness; those of the irascible: hope, despair, courage, fear, anger and satisfaction.
>
> Also to be considered in the heart are: affections, sentiments, tendencies and inclinations.[21]

The concupiscible passions are directly related to good and evil. The irascible passions are related to good and evil under the aspect of difficulty.[22]

Whether we speak of passions or emotions, the same is true for both: one must not allow them to lead. For example, one is not to allow his emotions to suddenly change his mind in the face of principles and reasoned decisions. When they are subject to the intellect and the will, emotions and passions enjoy a controlled freedom, and good and evil take on the correct perspective.

It is always possible to exercise control over one's emotions by directing the mind to something else that will hold its attention. Emotions will settle without the attention of the mind. Sometimes it is easier to remove the cause that stimulated the emotion, or to remove oneself from the stimulus or occasion.

The solution to the problem of emotions and passions, then, is intelligent control. Controlled emotions can have a healthy effect on one's spiritual life. For example, emotions of disgust or aversion for sin counteract one's attraction to sin.

Passions play an important role in everyone's life. They influence physical activity, bodily health, and ideals. They increase or diminish human responsibility, merit or demerit, for good or evil actions.

The most perfect example of right-ordered emotions is the Divine Master Himself. He marveled at the faith of the centurion (Mt. 8:10)*; He was distressed at the lack of faith shown by the people of Nazareth (Mk. 6:6)*; He was deeply moved by the heartbreak of Martha and Mary over the death of Lazarus (Jn. 11:33)*; He showed rightful indignation over the buying and selling that was taking place in the Temple (Mt. 21:12).* Christ loved children, the poor, the sick, His disciples and apostles, and He showed His love exteriorly. Jesus' teachings were effective because they came from the depths of His heart, and for this reason, they penetrated the hearts of those who listened. The people were persuaded by the

Divine Master's teachings because they knew that He lived what He taught.

In his encyclical *Divini illius Magistri,* Pope Pius XI outlines the task of catechesis regarding the affective aspect of Christian formation:

> There remain in human nature the effects of original sin, the chief of which are weakness of will and disorderly inclinations. Disorderly inclinations then must be corrected, good tendencies encouraged and regulated, and above all the mind must be enlightened and the will strengthened by supernatural truth and by the means of grace, without which it is impossible to control evil impulses, impossible to attain complete and full perfection.[23]

Father Alberione emphasizes:

> In order to dominate our heart, God's grace is needed. And with the grace of God the heart is directed toward Him. God is Supreme Love: we must love Him with all our heart! Grace is a gift of God, supernatural, ordered to eternal salvation. This gift divinizes man, as it is written: "You are sons of the Most High" (Ps. 18:6), and elsewhere: "Through grace you have become partakers of the divine nature" (cf. 2 Pt. 1:4).
>
> It consists, therefore, in a new principle of life, which effects a supernatural transformation in man. Grace is absolutely necessary.[24]

As the means of grace, we have the Liturgy, which is our life of worship. In worship, the doctrine grasped by the intellect, accepted by the will and applied to daily life is expressed through one's sentiments and interior dispositions. The

Eucharistic Celebration, the sacraments, prayer and especially the reception of the Holy Eucharist are the sources of grace, the sources of the soul's supernatural life.

> Therefore, catechesis must promote an active, conscious, genuine participation in the liturgy of the Church, not merely by explaining the meaning of the ceremonies, but also by forming the minds of the faithful for prayer, for thanksgiving, for repentance, for praying with confidence, for a community spirit, and for understanding correctly the meaning of the creeds. All these things are necessary for a true liturgical life (GCD, 25).

The theological virtue of charity has a particular relationship to the affective life. It intimately unites a person with God. The object of his love is God as the Supreme Good and Ultimate End. A person loves himself and his neighbor for love of God. With an increase of the virtue of charity that comes by practice, and through an increase of sanctifying grace, our heart is directed to God, and everyone else, and everything else is loved in view of love for God.

> Love of God is the soul of morality.... Sustained by faith, man is to live a life of love of God and of his fellow men. This is his greatest responsibility, and the source of his greatest dignity. A man's holiness, whatever his vocation or state of life may be, is the perfection of love of God (BT, 18).

Father Alberione states:

> It is all important that the subjects we study, the truths we penetrate, the moral teachings we

learn and the liturgy in which we participate, inflame our hearts and produce love.[25]

Christian life is the realization of the Redemption in souls. It is the application to man of the redemptive work of Jesus the Divine Master. It is the cooperation of man with Jesus Christ through a life of faith, hope and charity.

Through faith the soul holds firmly to God, the very source of truth. Through hope the soul desires Him, the source of happiness. Through charity the soul is united, together with Jesus, to God, Who is Love.

Following Jesus Christ, the Way, the Truth and the Life, man will give perfect worship to God: faith in the mind, submission in the will, love in the heart—to know God, to serve Him, to love Him.

Jesus Christ the Divine Master is Truth for the intellect, Way for the will, and Life for the sentiments of the heart.

FORMATION OF THE WHOLE PERSON IN CHRIST THROUGH THE WAY, TRUTH AND LIFE METHOD

CHRIST:	TRUTH	WAY	LIFE
	↓	↓	↓
	Creed	Code	Cult
	|	|	|
	Doctrine	Gospel Morality	Liturgy/ Private Prayer
	|	|	|
	Truths of Faith	Commandments	Sacraments/ Grace
	↓	↓	↓
CHURCH:	Teaches	Guides	Sanctifies
	↓	↓	↓
PERSON:	Mind	Will	Heart
	|	|	|
	Cognitive Powers	Volitional Powers	Affective Powers
	|	|	|
	Intellectual level	Behavioral level	Emotional level

FOOTNOTES—CHAPTER TWO

1. The Aramaic is rendered Rabbi (my master); the Greek, Didaskalos; the Latin, Magister; the Italian, Maestro; and the English, Teacher, although it does not suggest the full significance of the title. Because "master" has acquired another connotation, "teacher" or "educator" seems more acceptable.

This writer uses the term "Master" as Jesus' title in the best sense: instructor, educator, model, and exemplar.

2. Alberione, "Regina Apostolorum" (internal circular of the Daughters of St. Paul) (Rome, 1959).

3. Alberione, *Istruzioni alle Maestre* (Rome: Figlie di San Paolo, 1936), p. 120.

4. Alberione, *To the Pauline Families* (Boston: Daughters of St. Paul, 1954), p. 26.

5. Alberione, *"Abundantes Divitiae Gratiae Suae,"* p. 53.

6. Ibid.

7. Ibid., p. 54.

8. Alberione, *Convegno Catechistico Paolino,* January, 1960 (Rome: Figlie di San Paolo, 1960), p. 4.

9. Alberione, "Jesus Master and Christian Formation," *Pauline Spirituality,* p. 167.

10. Pope Pius XI, "Divini illius Magistri," *Education: Papal Teachings* (Boston: St. Paul Editions, 1960), pp. 168, 227, 203.

11. Alberione, *Convegno Catechistico Paolino,* p. 5.

12. Cf. Alberione, *Spiritual Exercises*, Ariccia, Italy, 1964 (tape recording).

13. Alberione, *Santificazione della Mente* (Rome: Edizioni Paoline, 1956), p. 14.

14. The writer does not intend to suggest methods for classroom presentation of doctrine. Her purpose is to point out that the faculties of the mind and will, and the affective powers of the heart, must be formed and developed through catechetical instruction if the total Christian is to be formed in Christ.

15. Cf. Pope John Paul II, Apostolic Exhortation *Catechesi tradendae* (Boston: St. Paul Editions, 1979, no. 20.

16. Alberione, *To the Pauline Families*, p. 133.

17. Ibid., p. 132.

18. Ibid.

19. Alberione, *Meditation on Christian Formation*, Haec Meditare, Serie Prima, vol. IV.

20. Some psychologists choose to use the word *passions* to indicate violent urgings of the sense appetite, and use the word *emotion*, instead, to indicate the more gentle and ordinary movements.

The purpose of catechesis, however, is to help the student control and direct *all* the movements of his affective aspect whether these are passions, emotions, sentiments or tendencies.

21. Alberione, *Pray Always* (Boston: St. Paul Editions, 1960), p. 19.

22. For a more extensive treatment of this subject, the writer suggests *Spiritual Theology* by Jordan Aumann, O.P., Our Sunday Visitor, Inc., Huntington, Indiana 46750.

23. Pius XI, "Divini illius Magistri," *Education: Papal Teachings*, p. 278

24. Alberione, *Pray Always*, p. 19.

25. Alberione, "Life Oriented to Jesus Master," *Pauline Spirituality*, p. 382.

III. "Anyone Who Loves Me Will Be True to My Word" (Jn. 14:23)*

Speaking for himself and the other apostles, Philip asked Jesus to show them the Father: "...show us the Father and that will be enough for us" (Jn. 14:8).* In reply, Jesus expressed His disappointment: "After I have been with you all this time, you still do not know me?" (Jn. 14:9)*

The knowledge that Jesus was referring to was not the knowledge of His physical person; this the apostles knew well. Jesus was speaking about an intimate, supernatural knowledge, a knowledge of His mission and of His doctrine, a knowledge of His spirit and of His heart. This is the knowledge that John referred to when he wrote:

Eternal life is this:
to know you, the only true God,
and him whom you have sent,
Jesus Christ (Jn. 17:3).*

It is the knowledge that leads to faith, like that of Peter when he confessed: "You are the Messiah, the Son of the living God!" (Mt. 16:16)*; or like that of Thomas when he exclaimed: "My Lord and my God!" (Jn. 20:28)* It is the knowledge that leads to love, to imitation and to life according to His spirit.

The purpose of man's existence on this earth is to know, love and serve God his Creator so that he might be happy with Him and possess Him for all eternity.

In His infinite wisdom and love, God created man for Himself and instilled in him three basic aspirations: the desire for happiness, the desire for truth, the desire for love. Man seeks to satisfy these desires through his primary faculties: the will strives for happiness, the intellect for truth. And the sentiments of the heart long for love. Each and all of man's desires find satisfaction in God alone. For this reason, man's faculties must be directed toward God. Because the mind, will and sentiments of the heart are to operate in harmony, they must be formed or directed equally. A stress on one or another can lead to a personality imbalance. The same holds true for Christian formation through catechesis. There must be equal emphasis on doctrine, morals, and liturgy in order to achieve a balanced formation of the mind, the will and the heart.

Father Alberione notes:

> A Christian is not well formed unless he has faith, unless his conduct conforms to evangelical morality, and unless he lives a supernatural life.[1]

From this statement we can easily conclude that knowledge alone of religious truths is insufficient. Religious instruction should be only a means to the goal which is religious living.

Joseph A. Jungmann, a great pioneer in twentieth century catechetics writes:

> Considered in its essence catechesis cannot be restricted solely to religious instruction, to doctrine, to something that need only be "known."
>
> Christian doctrine can never be an end in itself; it must direct us to God. Knowledge is necessary, but it is a knowledge of that way which we must traverse. Catechesis must be religious-moral direction.[2]

A living faith, or doctrine applied to life, is not an innovation or a new method that has developed in the last century with the catechetical renewal. The very nature of Christianity demands this correlation. The teachings of the Divine Master, whether they be His words or His actions, can never be separated from His life. "The whole of Christ's life was a continual teaching..." (CT, 9). That He expects us to translate our beliefs into practice is evident from His exhortations: "Anyone who hears my words and puts them into practice is like the wise man who built his house on rock" (Mt. 7:24).* "None of those who cry out, 'Lord, Lord,' will enter the kingdom of God but only the one who does the will of my Father in heaven" (Mt. 7:21).* A truth that has not been incorporated into one's life and put into practice is like a barren tree. "Every tree that is not fruitful will be cut down and thrown into the fire" (Mt. 3:10).* The Divine Master expresses this same idea more forcefully in the parable of the talents:

> You wicked and lazy servant! So you knew that I reap where I have not sown and gather where I have not scattered? Well then, you should have deposited my money with the bankers, and on my return I would have recovered my capital with interest. So now, take the talent from him...throw him out into the dark, where there will be weeping and grinding of teeth (Mt. 25:26-30).*

The letters of St. Paul were addressed to persons who were already familiar with the Gospel. Although some doctrines are mentioned occasionally, his letters, for the most part, present the application of doctrine to everyday life: "Live according to what you have learned and accepted, what you have heard me say and seen me do" (Phil. 4:9).* "Whatever you do, whether in speech or in action, do it in the name of the Lord Jesus" (Col. 3:17).* "My point is that you should live in accord with the spirit and you will not yield to the cravings of the flesh" (Gal. 5:16).* "There was a time when you were darkness, but now you are light in the Lord. Well, then, live as children of light" (Eph. 5:8).*

St. James has given us the most straightforward presentation of the relationship between dogmatic truths and daily life:

> My brothers, what good is it to profess faith without practicing it? Such faith has no power to save one, has it? If a brother or sister has nothing to wear and no food for the day, and you say to them,

"Good-bye and good luck! Keep warm and well fed," but do not meet their bodily needs, what good is that? So it is with the faith that does nothing in practice. It is thoroughly lifeless (Jas. 2:14-17).*

Considering these passages from Sacred Scripture, we may conclude that Revelation has not been given to us only for the enlightenment of our intellect but also, and what seems to be more important, for the transformation of our life.

The *General Catechetical Directory* states:

> Catechesis performs the function of disposing men to receive the action of the Holy Spirit and to deepen their conversion. It does this through the word, to which are joined the witness of life and prayer (GCD, 22).

In describing the "Task of the Catechist," Jungmann writes:

> The life of grace as a seed, which is implanted in the soul of the child at Baptism, must ultimately unfold into a well-rounded Christian life. The power of faith must be channelled into action; it must be fostered into a believing acceptance of the divine message of "good news." From faith, hope must spring up, and from hope, love, the wholehearted and ardent turning to God, the Supreme Good. Through the moral virtues the right attitude toward earthly things must be found: a conviction, a resolution, a holy resolve. This objective may sometimes be also a sentiment, a joy about God's might and God's ways, a prayer, a hymn, in any case not simply knowledge.[3]

St. Pius X, who we can say inaugurated the catechetical renewal within the Church, stressed:

> The task of the catechist is to take up one or other of the truths of faith or of Christian morality and then explain it in all its parts; and since amendment of life is the chief aim of his instruction, the catechist must needs make a comparison between what God commands us to do and what is our actual conduct.[4]

In addressing catechists, Father Jungmann also reminded them of the necessity to apply doctrine to life:

> As a teacher the catechist must always bear in mind that his task is not simply to imprint upon the minds of the children a great number of theoretical statements without paying any heed to their meaning or connection with one another. He must rather introduce the children to the supernatural world of faith in such a way that the momentous thoughts that are embraced by it become those ideals by which they can orientate themselves and by which they can be guided on life's highway, and that these ideals evolve into powerful virtues which will propel them along the ways of Christian living.[5]

In its first years, the catechetical renewal movement stressed methods above all. Its aim in this regard was to improve religious instruction by relating it more closely to daily living.

Father Johannes Hofinger, S.J., promoter of the "kerygmatic renewal" in catechetics explains:

> The modern catechetical movement originated chiefly as a much needed reaction against the

intellectualism which, toward the end of the nineteenth century, was severely endangering the teaching of religion. While the importance of religious knowledge was overemphasized, religious formation and religious living were unintentionally neglected. Teachers all too often were content to have their students merely memorize the catechism; they sacrificed true understanding to mechanical drill. But even where true understanding was the aim, and an aim which was achieved to a high degree, the heart and its education were still neglected. In contrast, the catechetical movement has emphasized what is the true educational function of our catechetical activity: we not only have to give our students a thorough knowledge of their faith but we must also form true Christians who truly live their Christianity.[6]

At the outset of the renewal, Pius X stated in his encyclical *Acerbo nimis* that "In matters of religion, the majority of men in our times must be considered uninstructed."[7] And, although the Church has continued her diligent efforts toward authentic catechetical renewal through her magisterial directives and exhortations, her voice has not always been heeded. As one of the consequences, the overemphasis on religious instruction, that was viewed as an imbalance has, it seems in our day, given way to an underemphasis on doctrine. So much is this the case that The *General Catechetical Directory* states:

> Great numbers are drifting little by little into religious indifferentism, or are continuing in danger of keeping the faith without the dynamism that is necessary, a faith without effective influence on

their actual lives. The question now is not one of merely preserving traditional religious customs, but rather one of also fostering an appropriate re-evangelization of men, obtaining their reconversion, and giving them a deeper and more mature education in the faith (GCD, 6).

The words of Pius XI have not lost their meaning or their impact:

> It is incredible how great is the ignorance of Christian Doctrine which the Church suffers in the present time. This is true of the faithful in whatever age group or social rank. Hence the Catechism must be given with renewed dedication, lest in a time of so much education in other fields, religious knowledge, the most important of all, alone suffer neglect.[8]

The root of the problem in our day, however, goes beyond the imbalances mentioned. The imbalances are a result of what The *General Catechetical Directory* has included in "The Reality of the Problem":

> Faulty opinions are being spread abroad with greater speed and are exerting an ever-wider influence among the faithful, young adults especially, who suffer grave crises and are not infrequently driven to adopt ways of acting and thinking that are hostile to religion (GCD, 5).

The Church has never been unaware of these "faulty opinions," nor has she ever hesitated to speak out and identify them, at the same time directing the faithful to the proper resolve.

In his encyclical letter *Aeterni Patris*, Leo XIII writes:

> ...since in the tempest that is on us the Christian faith is being constantly assailed by the machinations and craft of a certain false wisdom, all youths, but especially those who are the growing hope of the Church, should be nourished on the strong and robust food of doctrine....[9]

Pope Pius X reminds the faithful that the Church must guard the deposit of faith entrusted to her by Christ:

> One of the primary obligations assigned by Christ to the office divinely committed to Us of feeding the Lord's flock is that of guarding with the greatest vigilance the deposit of the faith delivered to the saints, rejecting the profane novelties of words and the gainsaying of knowledge falsely so called. There has never been a time when this watchfulness of the supreme pastor was not necessary to the Catholic body, for owing to the efforts of the enemy of the human race, there have never been lacking "men speaking perverse things," "vain talkers and seducers," "erring and driving into error."
>
> ...We may no longer keep silence, lest We should seem to fail in Our most sacred duty.[10]

In his encyclical letter, St. Pius X describes each of the so-called "doctrines" of the Modernists. The errors stated have, in some way, infiltrated into the various branches of learning; however, this writer has selected two in particular to illustrate their direct bearing on catechesis.

"Evolution of dogma": the modernist holds that dogma is not only able to evolve, but that it ought to evolve and be changed. If "religious formulas" are really "religious," that is, springing from a religious sense or the need of a soul for the divine, and not merely intellectual speculations, then they ought to be living, and living the life of the religious sense. The religious sense assimilates the "dogma," accepts it and sanctions it by the heart. In order to be living and remain living, the formulas should be adapted to the believer. If for any reason they lose their adaptation, they lose their meaning and need to be changed.[11]

If by any chance this prevarication could be true, then truth would be relative and subjective rather than absolute and objective. Truth would not be truth. God would not be God. Then reality would be what an individual would want it to be —and this is ludicrous.

"Deformation of religious history": the faith that has sprung from the "religious sense" is attracted by the unknowable which is united to the phenomenon. This faith permeates and transfigures the phenomenon by elevating it above its true conditions. This results in a certain disfiguration of the phenomenon and this disfiguration takes place especially in the case of the phenomenon of the past.[12]

The Person of Christ serves as an example.

> In the Person of Christ, they say, science and history encounter nothing that is not human. Therefore...whatever there is in His history suggestive of the divine must be rejected.... The historical Perso

of Christ was transfigured by faith; therefore everything that raises it above historical conditions must be removed…. The Person of Christ…disfigured by faith, requires that everything should be excluded, deeds and words and all else, that is not in strict keeping with His character, condition, and education, and with the place and time in which He lived.[13]

As a result of this false reasoning, the Jesus of history is disassociated from the Christ of the Gospel.

In his encyclical letter *Humani generis*, Pope Pius XII again outlines these false opinions which threaten to undermine the foundations of Catholic doctrine. He does not hesitate to point out the eagerness for novelty on the part of some teachers:

…We know that Catholic teachers generally avoid these errors; it is apparent, however, that some today, as in apostolic times, desirous of novelty and fearing to be considered ignorant of recent scientific findings, try to withdraw themselves from the sacred Teaching Authority and are accordingly in danger of gradually departing from revealed truth and of drawing others along with them into error.[14]

Again, in 1964, through the Instruction of the Pontifical Biblical Commission, *The Historicity of the Gospels*, the Church expressed her concern over the many writings in circulation which question the truth of the events and sayings reported in the Gospels.[15] The document directly states the erroneous premises on which some exegetes base their "form criticism."

> Some...motivated by rationalistic prejudices, refuse to recognize the existence of a supernatural order. They deny the intervention of a personal God in the world by means of Revelation in the strict sense, and reject the possibility or actual occurrence of miracles and prophecies. Some start out with an erroneous concept of faith, regarding faith as indifferent to, or even incompatible with, historical truth. Some deny, *a priori* as it were, the historical nature and historical value of the documents of Revelation. And finally, some minimize the authority of the Apostles as witnesses to Christ. Belittling their office and their influence in the primitive community, these people exaggerate the creative power of the community itself.[16]

The document goes on to point out that these opinions are contrary to Catholic doctrine and devoid of scholarly foundation.

In each of the documents issued by the Magisterium, the Church's concern for purity of doctrine and preservation of the deposit of faith is evident. Jesus Christ is the focal point of this sacred deposit. He is the center of the Gospel message within salvation history. In Him the Church has its foundation (cf. GCD, 40).

To any who might contradict or disregard the teachings of Christ, Father Alberione counsels:

> The Divine Master preached His doctrine, but what was mankind's reaction? Mankind should have received the word of heaven, but just the opposite occurred. Many refused to listen to Him, not only when He spoke visibly on earth, but also down through the centuries that followed. Opposi-

tion against the doctrine preached by the apostles has been continuous. Jesus has become the center of contradiction, and we hear many teachers who raise their voices and seek to make themselves heard through all the means at their disposal, to contradict the Church. By so doing they contradict Jesus Christ Himself.

The words of Christ are without compromise, "He who believes and is baptized will be saved; he who does not believe will be condemned" (Mk. 16:16).**[17]

For the same reason that Christ is the central fact of the history of mankind, He is also the central figure of catechesis, as Pope John Paul II exhorts:

> The primary and essential object of catechesis is, to use an expression dear to St. Paul and also to contemporary theology, "the mystery of Christ." Catechizing is in a way to lead a person to study this mystery in all its dimensions... (CT, 5).

> Christocentricity in catechesis also means the intention to transmit not one's own teaching or that of some other master, but the teaching of Jesus Christ, the Truth that He communicates or, to put it more precisely, the Truth that He is (CT, 6).

The point of importance, then, is that Jesus Christ is the content of catechesis. He is the focal point of salvation history (cf. GCD, 41), the subject and the object of Revelation. Acting in conformity with His commandments, the Christian sets himself to follow Christ (cf. CT, 20). The sacraments are the actions of Christ in the Church (cf. GCD,

55) and flow from His life-giving grace. In the sacraments, especially in the Eucharist, Christ Jesus works in fullness for the transformation of human beings (cf. CT, 23). The liturgy is an exercise of the priestly office of Jesus Christ (cf. SC, 7).

It stands to reason, then, that in catechesis the emphasis should be on the Person of Christ Who, through His life and teachings, gave us a doctrine, that is, a body of truths to be believed and precepts to be obeyed. That He intended His doctrine to be taught and His precepts to be obeyed is evident:

> Full authority has been given to me
> both in heaven and on earth;
> go, therefore, and make disciples of all the nations....
> Teach them to carry out everything I have commanded you (Mt. 28:18-20).*

The fullness of revelation which is contained in the teachings and in the life of Jesus is meant to be a part of each person's life experience. But still, no experience could ever adequately express the universal value of Christ's message, because experience is restricted by situations. For this reason, experience cannot replace or oppose a systematic study of that doctrine which is universal.

John Paul II explains:

> It is useless to play off orthopraxis against orthodoxy: Christianity is inseparably both. Firm and well-thought-out convictions lead to courageous and upright action; the endeavor to educate the faithful to live as disciples of Christ today calls

for and facilitates a discovery in depth of the mystery of Christ in the history of salvation.

It is also quite useless to campaign for the abandonment of serious and orderly study of the message of Christ in the name of a method concentrating on life experience. "No one can arrive at the whole truth on the basis solely of some private experience, that is to say, without an adequate explanation of the message of Christ, who is 'the way, and the truth, and the life' (Jn. 14:6)"

Nor is any opposition to be set up between a catechesis taking life as its point of departure and a traditional doctrinal and systematic catechesis. Authentic catechesis is always an orderly and systematic initiation into the revelation that God has given of Himself to humanity in Christ Jesus, a revelation stored in the depths of the Church's memory and in Sacred Scripture, and constantly communicated from one generation to the next by a living, active *traditio* (CT, 22).

The *Traditio Symboli* (transmission of the summary of the faith) has been the most important stage in the life of Christ's disciples because this summary of the essential truths to be believed is the point of departure for a more profound and a more faithful following of Christ.

For this reason, Paul VI wrote:

> The intelligence, especially that of children and young people, needs to learn through systematic religious instruction the fundamental teachings, the living content of the truth which God has wished to convey to us and which the Church has sought to express in an ever richer fashion during the course of her long history. No one will deny that this

instruction must be given to form patterns of Christian living and not to remain only notional (EN, 44).

There can be no doubt that a deep knowledge of Christ works to give meaning and hope to daily existence. The Gospel is truly the leaven of liberty and progress in human history, the leaven of brotherhood, unity and peace (cf. AG, 8).

In addressing the members of a Symposium held at St. John's University (Jamaica, N.Y.) to celebrate the second anniversary of *Catechesi tradendae*, Cardinal Silvio Oddi, Prefect of the Sacred Congregation for the Clergy, stated:

> The result of eclectic glimpses of Jesus is to set in false opposition life experience and catechetical content, method and spontaneity, morality and freedom, memory and understanding. Such antitheses are artificial and will not arise if the *whole* Jesus is presented to the faithful, but they will, of course, inevitably appear if Jesus is shown as merely the perfect man rather than the Divine Son of Mary, the Word made flesh.[18]

His Eminence further clarified the necessity of using the Christological approach if catechesis is to be authentic.

> ...using the Christological approach...namely to present a balanced, integral Christian message, we shall immediately be able to identify and avoid most of the present day catechetical excesses, which generally result from minimizing or even excluding from catechesis those qualities of Our Lord seen to be incompatible with novelties favored by this or

that fashionable theological school. We must receive Jesus and preach Jesus exactly as the Father sent Him to us, and doctrinal fads which distort the real Jesus must be avoided like the proverbial plague.[19]

The primacy of orthodoxy in catechesis does not eliminate "the witness of an authentic Christian life given over to God" (EN, 41).

Because authentic catechesis must lead the individual to communion with the Person and life of Jesus, there is as much need of orthodoxy as orthopraxis. Opposition between the two would alter the nature of catechesis at its center: Jesus the Divine Master, Way, Truth and Life.

FOOTNOTES—CHAPTER THREE

1. Alberione, *Ritiro di Gennaio*, Haec Meditare, Serie Prima, vol. IV.
2. Joseph A. Jungmann, *Handing on the Faith* (New York: Herder and Herder, 1962), p. 92.
3. Ibid., pp. 92-93.
4. Pius X, *Acerbo nimis, On the Teaching of Christian Doctrine*, trans. Joseph B. Collins (Boston: St. Paul Editions, 1979), p. 9.
5. Jungmann, *Handing on the Faith*, p. 94.
6. Johannes Hofinger, S.J., *The Good News and Its Proclamation* (Notre Dame, Ind.: University of Notre Dame Press, 1968), p. 23.
7. Pius X, *Acerbo nimis*, p. 13.
8. Pius XI, "Letter to the Cardinal Archbishop of Naples," AAS (1928), pp. 290-291.
9. Leo XIII, *Aeterni Patris* (Boston: St. Paul Editions, 1979), p. 19.
10. Pius X, *Pascendi Dominici gregis, On the Doctrine of the Modernists* (Boston: St. Paul Editions, 1977), p. 7.
11. Cf. Ibid., p. 17.
12. Cf. Ibid., p. 13.
13. Ibid., p. 14.
14. Pope Pius XII, *Humani generis* (Boston: St. Paul Editions, 1956), pp. 3-4.
15. Cf. Pontifical Biblical Commission, *The Historicity of the Gospels* (Boston: St. Paul Editions, 1981), p. 3.
16. Ibid., p. 5.
17. Alberione, "Unpublished Hour of Adoration," *Pauline Spirituality*, p. 535.
18. Cardinal Silvio Oddi, "Jesus Christ Is the Message," *L'Osservatore Romano*, English Weekly Edition, June 22, 1981, p. 4.
19. Ibid.

IV. "I Came from the Father and Have Come into the World"
(Jn. 16:28)*

The Divine Master first revealed Himself in the creation of the world, then in Sacred Scripture through the prophets, and in the fullness of time, by speaking to mankind directly and communicating His heavenly wisdom. Jesus Christ continues to speak to men through the Church, through that Church founded by Him, which interprets His revelation and teaches mankind throughout the ages.

Jesus lives undiminished only in that Church which has written and preached the Scriptures; in that Church wherein apostolic tradition remains alive in Christian hearts: in that Church which celebrates the sacraments, proclaims the creeds, assembles the councils, worships the Father, offers the Body of the Lord in her liturgy, and lives by the unfailing Spirit of God. The Church is alive in Christ and Christ lives in His Church.[1]

Father Alberione urges:

> We must turn to the Church and let ourselves be guided by her, because the Church takes from Jesus Christ and communicates the truth to us.[2]

Christocentric catechesis is not a new or recent development in catechetical methodology. Beginning with the apostolic age, the Church has always presented Christ-centered doctrine, Christ-centered living. The application of the Way, Truth and Life method in catechetics is a continuation of that same Christ-centered catechesis, and the continuation of the Church's teaching pattern of doctrine, morals and liturgy. It is doctrine applied to life and expressed through prayer.

The mandate of Christ, "Go..., make disciples of all the nations...baptize them...teach them..." (cf. Mt. 28:19, 20), directed the entire life and activity of the apostles. They were sent by Christ, the One sent by the Father. Jesus and the Father are One, so Jesus reveals the Father and the Father's will. The apostles were to announce to all nations and peoples the will of the Father revealed in Jesus Christ.

The apostles were sent; they were chosen (cf. Jn. 15:16). It was not their own initiative but a mission; they were empowered: "Full authority has been given to me...go, therefore..." (Mt. 28:18, 19).*

The Father sent the Son, and the Son in turn chose His disciples whom He sent. By their life and mission they continued the work of the Son.

The presentation of the Gospel message is not an optional contribution of the Church. It is the duty incumbent on her by the command of the Lord Jesus, so that people can believe and be saved (EN, 5).

To be faithful to one's calling and to the mission entrusted to him, the apostle, or the "one who is sent," must remain united with the one who sends. In this regard, it is Jesus Christ. Authentic catechesis, then, presupposes fidelity to the mission received and the message proclaimed.

Catechesis must proclaim Jesus in His concrete existence and in His message, that is, it must open the way for men to the wonderful perfection of His humanity in such a way that they will be able to acknowledge the mystery of His divinity....

Catechesis ought daily to defend and strengthen belief in the divinity of Jesus Christ, in order that He may be accepted not merely for His admirable human life, but that men might recognize Him through His words and signs as God's only-begotten Son (GCD, 53).

In the Acts of the Apostles we have a description of the first Christian community: "They devoted themselves to the apostles' instruction and the communal life, to the breaking of bread and the prayers" (Acts 2:42).* The apostles, who were taught by the Divine Master, are His faithful witnesses and can transmit His doctrine and explain the meaning of His life, death and resurrection. The core of the apostles' instruction is Peter's discourse on the day of Pentecost (Acts

2:22-39).* The Acts also records another discourse of Peter (Acts 3:12-26),* but the message—that is, the instruction—is the same.

Both in the Acts of the Apostles and in their letters, it is clear that the apostles intended to teach, and that the content of their teaching was Jesus Christ. "Day after day, both in the temple and at home, they never stopped teaching and proclaiming the good news of Jesus the Messiah" (Acts 5:42).* It can be especially noted in the Letter to the Hebrews that there was an initial instruction. "Let us, then, go beyond the initial teaching about Christ and advance to maturity, not laying the foundation all over again..." (Heb. 6:1).* In the First Letter of St. Paul to the Corinthians, we again find the content for the initial instruction:

> Brothers, I want to remind you of the gospel I preached to you, which you received and in which you stand firm. You are being saved by it at this very moment if you hold fast to it as I preached it to you. Otherwise you have believed in vain. I handed on to you first of all what I myself received, that Christ died for our sins in accordance with the Scriptures; that he was buried and, in accordance with the Scriptures, rose on the third day; that he was seen by Cephas, then by the Twelve. After that he was seen by five hundred brothers at once, most of whom are still alive, although some have fallen asleep. Next he was seen by James; then by all the apostles. Last of all he was seen by me, as one born out of the normal course (1 Cor. 15:1-8).*

All of the letters of the apostles are significantly catechetical (cf. CT, 11). They build on an initial instruction, and deepen this instruction while they guard the original deposit of faith and make certain that this deposit is handed on unimpaired.

The words of Paul to Timothy reflect this concern:

> O Timothy, guard what has been committed to you (1 Tm. 6:20).*

> The things which you have heard from me... you must hand on to trustworthy men who will be able to teach others (2 Tm. 2:2).*

Here we note that:

> The apostles were not slow to share with others the ministry of apostleship. They transmitted to their successors the task of teaching (CT, 11).

The Church continued to carry out the mission that had been entrusted to the apostles and their successors. Apostolic catechesis took on a definite form and structure, and the deposit of faith remained the core of catechetical instruction.

Through their writings, the Fathers of the Church transmitted the basics of the faith, and for this reason they can all be considered catechists.

The writings of the early Fathers bear testimony that the deposit or "rule" of faith is the instrument and means for Christian catechesis.

The *Didaché* or "The Teaching," dated toward the end of the first century, represents the Church's earliest form of catechetical instruction. It presents the doctrine of the two ways: the way of life is the way of the Gospel precepts and the virtues to be practiced; the way of death, the vices to be avoided. This instruction also contains a liturgical summary of Baptism, prayer and the Eucharist, as well as a broad outline of Church organization. The unknown author points out to the community of believers which teachers or catechists they are to accept and which they are to reject:

> Accordingly, when an itinerant teaches you all that has been said, welcome him. But should the teacher himself be a turncoat and teach a different doctrine so as to undermine (this teaching), do not listen to him. But if he promotes holiness and knowledge of the Lord, welcome him as the Lord."[3]

Proof of the Apostolic Preaching was written by St. Irenaeus (end of the second century), the Bishop of Lyons. It is a short catechetical treatise—a summary of the principal truths of faith—addressed to a certain Marcianus in order to:

> ...set forth in brief the preaching of the truth, to confirm your faith...so that you may find much matter in short space, comprehending in a few details all the members of the body of truth, and receiving in brief the proof of the things of God. In this way, not only will it bear fruit in your salvation, but also you may confound all those who hold false views, and to all who wish to hear, you may with all confidence expound what we have to say in its integrity and purity.[4]

The fundamental points of the "rule of faith" are developed: namely, the three major articles of the Creed—the doctrine of the Father (creation), of the Son (redemption), and of the Holy Spirit (sanctification of mankind).

This *Proof of the Apostolic Preaching* is the earliest resumé we have of Christian doctrine, but it is also apologetic in nature since it is a "proof" of the apostolic preaching. Acceptance of the truths stated therein is acceptance of the true Church founded by Jesus Christ on the apostles.

> This, beloved, is the preaching of the truth, and this is the manner of our salvation, and this is the way of life, announced by the prophets and ratified by Christ and handed over by the Apostles and handed down by the Church in the whole world to her children. This must be kept in all security with good will, and by being well pleasing to God through good works and sound moral character.[5]

The major concern of Irenaeus was to preserve the catechumenate[6] from Gnostic influence; therefore, *The Proof* must be studied in the light of his major work *Adversus Haereses*, "Against the Heresies." For the Gnostics, Jesus was one among many teachers. But in the catechumenate, Jesus Christ is the one, true Teacher—the Word of God Incarnate. This work, profoundly theological, clearly supports Christocentric catechesis. The teachers in the catechumenate are to see Jesus Christ as the only true Teacher. Jesus Christ *is* the rule of faith.

> But follow the only true and steadfast Teacher, the Word of God, our Lord Jesus Christ, who did, through His transcendent love, become what we are, that He might bring us to be even what He is Himself (Bk. 5, Preface).

> As I have already observed, the Church, having received this preaching and this faith, although

> scattered throughout the whole world, yet, as if occupying but one house, carefully preserves it. She also believes these points of doctrine just as if she had but one soul, and one and the same heart, and she proclaims them, and teaches them, and hands them down, with perfect harmony, as if she possessed only one mouth. For, although the languages of the world are dissimilar, yet the import of the tradition is one and the same (Bk. 1, Chap. 10, 2).

> But there is one only God, the Creator.... He is the God of Abraham, and the God of Isaac, and the God of Jacob, the God of the living; He it is whom the law proclaims, whom the prophets preach, whom Christ reveals, whom the apostles make known to us, and in whom the Church believes. He is the Father of our Lord Jesus Christ: through His Word, who is His Son, through Him He is revealed and manifested to all to whom He *is* revealed; for those only know Him to whom the Son has revealed Him (Bk. 2, Chap. 90, 9).[7]

In the writings of Irenaeus the articles of the Creed are already evident. We can also note another point: the "rule of faith," which is the baptismal creed, is communicated in the teaching program of the Church.

The *Catechetical Lectures* of St. Cyril of Jerusalem were given orally, and what has come down to us in writing is a type of transcript rather than an actual manuscript. The lectures contain eighteen pre-baptismal discourses delivered to the "illuminandi" and five delivered to the "neophytes," the newly baptized. In these lectures we also see the continuity of the Church's teaching.

First, then, let there be laid as a firm foundation in your souls the doctrine concerning God: That God is One alone, unbegotten, without beginning, immutable, unchangeable; neither begotten by another, nor having any successor to His life; who neither began to live in time, nor shall ever have an end.... There is One God alone...the Father of One only before all ages, of One only, His Only-begotten Son, our Lord Jesus Christ, through whom He made all things visible and invisible (Catechesis IV, 4).

The Church is called Catholic because it is spread throughout the world, from end to end of the earth; also because it teaches universally and completely all the doctrines which man should know concerning things visible and invisible, heavenly and earthly; and because it subjects to right worship all mankind, rulers and ruled, lettered and unlettered; further because it treats and heals universally every sort of sin committed by soul and body, and it possesses in itself every conceivable virtue, whether in deeds, words or in spiritual gifts of every kind (Catechesis XVIII, 23).[8]

St. Cyril teaches the same truths as each of the Fathers who preceded him. He explains the articles of the Creed, then Christian morality, prayer and the sacramental life. This is the handing on of the "deposit of faith."

The Great Catechism, "Oratio catechetica magna," was written by Gregory of Nyssa explicitly for those teachers who instructed the catechumens. He states the reason for his work in the Prologue:

The presiding ministers of the "mystery of godliness" have need of a *system in their instructions*, in order that the Church may be replenished by the accession of such as should be saved, through the teaching of the word of faith being brought home to the hearing of unbelievers.[9]

In this synthesis of Christian doctrine, we find the fundamental articles of the Creed explained and defended with rational arguments. From this we can note that catechists were expected to know the content of "the rule of faith" as well as the reasons to support their teachings and their belief.

The major portion of this "catechism" is centered on the redemption of man accomplished by Jesus Christ.

The First Catechetical Instruction, "De Catechizandis Rudibus," of St. Augustine is a concrete example of how to teach catechism. The purpose of his work is stated at the outset: "how suitably to present that truth, the belief in which makes us Christians."[10] Augustine provides the Deacon and Catechist Deogratias with a treatise that is both theoretical (methods of instruction) and practical (two model instructions). He suggests that Deogratias use certain facts, events and passages from the Old Testament to show how God planned man's salvation. Thus, Salvation History is Christ-centered. The method Augustine demonstrates is very much the method Christ Himself used with those disciples on the way to Emmaus.

In this treatise of St. Augustine, the Patristic Age has left us with a work that is both catechetical and pedagogical. Augustine uses Sacred Scripture as the source of catechetical instruction, and so we can note that "the rule of faith" is Scripture-based.

In the Patristic literature of the Golden Age the catechumenate took on a definite structure. Four aspects can be noted: the content of catechetical instruction was always the twelve articles of the baptismal creed. Sacramental life was Christocentric with emphasis on the Real Presence. Gospel morality was explained within the framework of the Ten Commandments and in the light of the New Law. The Our Father was the outline used to teach prayer because it was the perfect prayer taught by Christ Himself.

When the Church had won victory over paganism, and Rome was Christian, the external structure of the catechumenate came to an end. Parents taught the elements of the faith to their children except during the more intense periods of sacramental preparation before reception of Holy Eucharist and Confirmation.

From approximately 500 A.D. to 1500 A.D., the catechumenate functioned through the ordinary and extraordinary Magisterium.

The sixteenth century brought a renewal of catechetical initiatives. The Council of Trent

> ...lies at the origin of the Roman Catechism, which is also known by the name of that council and which is a work of the first rank as a summary of Christian teaching and traditional theology for use by priests (CT, 13).

Because it is basically a pastoral directory, the Roman Catechism is to be used as a guide for preaching and for catechesis. The division of content reflects the teaching program of the catechumenate: the Creed, the Sacraments, the Decalogue and the Lord's Prayer.

Particularly significant is a statement in the "Introductory," calling for a catechesis that is centered on a knowledge of Christ and a following of His teachings:

> A teacher in the Church should, therefore, use his best endeavors that the faithful earnestly desire *to know Jesus Christ, and Him crucified,* that they be firmly convinced, and with the most heartfelt piety and devotion believe, that *there is no other name under heaven given to men, whereby we must be saved....*[11]

Because of its certain, yet balanced, non-controversial approach to the truths of faith, the Roman Catechism enjoys an ongoing relevance as an instrument of the ordinary Magisterium.

In 1742, Benedict XIV issued a major catechetical encyclical letter, *Etsi minime,* again manifesting the Church's concern for the deposit of faith. The encyclical confirms the directives of Trent, strongly recommends the use of the little Catechism written by St. Robert Bellarmine as the text in Christian doctrine classes, and initiates the laity into the catechetical apostolate.

From a catechetical perspective, Vatican Council I (1869-1870) promulgated two important documents: the dogmatic constitution *Dei Filius,* "On the Catholic Faith," and the dogmatic constitution *Pastor Aeternus,* "On the Church of Christ." Both of these documents have a direct bearing on catechetical instruction: the first confirms the nature of Divine Revelation, the primary object of which is

Jesus Christ; the second establishes the infallibility of the Supreme Magisterium, which is the channel of Revelation.

At the very outset of the twentieth century, Leo XIII issued an encyclical *On Jesus Christ Our Redeemer* (Nov. 1, 1900) which, when considered from a catechetical point of view, demonstrates the Christ-centered thought of the Church and her constant preoccupation, so to speak, that all may come to a knowledge and love of Jesus Christ.

> The whole object of Christian doctrine and morality is that "we being dead to sin, should live to justice" (1 Pt. 2:24)—that is, to virtue and holiness. In this consists the moral life, with the certain hope of a happy eternity. This justice, in order to be advantageous to salvation, is nourished by Christian faith. "The just man lives by faith" (Gal. 3:11). "Without faith it is impossible to please God" (Heb. 11:6). Consequently Jesus Christ, the Creator and Preserver of faith, also preserves and nourishes our moral life. This He does chiefly by the ministry of His Church.[12]

During the pontificate of Pope Pius X, catechesis enjoyed particular consideration. His encyclical letter *Acerbo nimis*, "On the Teaching of Christian Doctrine" (April 15, 1905), evidences his personal experience as a catechist. He emphasizes the primacy of catechesis in the Church's mission:

> ...the first duty of all those who are entrusted in any way with the government of the Church is to instruct the faithful in the things of God.... For a priest there is no duty more grave or obligation more binding than this.[13]

Pius X then outlined practical norms for the reorganization of parish catechesis.

Quam singulari, also issued by Pius X, settled the topic of Confession and First Communion of Catholic children and sparked an ongoing renewal in the sacramental life of all Catholics.

Pius XI carried on the program of his predecessor and coordinated catechesis on all levels through organization.

With the decree *Provido sane consilio* (1935) the erection of diocesan catechetical offices was prescribed. Pius XI also issued another important encyclical letter, *Divini illius Magistri*, "On Christian Education of Youth" (1929) which outlines the Church's principles regarding the education of the whole person in Christ:

> The proper and immediate aim of Christian education is to cooperate with divine grace in forming the true and perfect Christian, that is, to form Christ in those regenerated by Baptism, according to the emphatic expression of the Apostle: "My little children, of whom I am in travail in birth, until Christ be formed in you" (Gal. 4:19). For the true Christian must live a supernatural life in Christ: "Christ Who is your life" (Col. 3:4), and display it in all his actions: "That the life also of Jesus be made manifest in our mortal flesh" (2 Cor. 4:11).[14]

Pope Pius XII upheld the concern of the Church for the deposit of faith, and his concern regarding Christian formation as well as religious instruction was evident from his many radio messages and allocutions.

> We turn now to point out the urgent need of a method of teaching catechism which is accurate and complete, and which, whilst not neglecting the help of memory and imagination, lays stress on reason and explains, for example, that the sincere and conscious act of faith is the most rational and reasonable human act. Give the young as organic a view as possible of Catholic teaching. Make them see in Christ One Who will satisfy their vital need of knowledge that is full, orderly and enlightening.[15]

The program of "aggiornamento" introduced by Vatican II *has* seen a renewal in the Church's effort to adapt her pastoral ministry to contemporary man.

Each of the sixteen documents of the Council can be examined from a catechetical perspective, but this is not our present purpose. It is sufficient to note that the real "aggiornamento" which the documents called for always directs the Christian to metanoia, an interior conversion—a turning from self with a turning toward Christ the Master.

Father Alberione rightly viewed the Council not only as a great historical fact but more especially as an opportunity for Christians to confront their lives with the life and teachings of the Divine Master.

> This Council (Vatican II) is the great, historical, religious fact of our time. It is an examen that Christianity is making of itself, a reflection on many points which can be reduced to three:
>
> a) How much is Christian life practiced today in conformity with the Gospel? In what way is this life lived in the world today? In what is it lacking? What means are to be adapted for a valid purifica-

tion and elevation in Jesus Christ the Master? "Be perfect as your heavenly Father is perfect." "Learn of me." *"I am the Way."*

b) How far has the doctrine of Jesus Christ been spread? With what acceptance and understanding? How has it been preserved in its wholeness and purity in the world? What are the means by which it can win all minds—in keeping with the mandate of Jesus Christ the Master to the Church: "Teach all men"? "This is eternal life, that they may know the one, true God, and him alone whom he has sent, Jesus Christ." *"I am the Truth."*

c) How and in what way do we pray in Christ and in the Church, "in spirit and in truth"? How and in what way do we produce the fruits of life and grace of true sons of God and His heirs, coheirs of Jesus Christ? How do we better our practical application of the words, "Our Father, who art in heaven, hallowed be Thy name; Thy kingdom come, Thy will be done"? What are the difficulties and improvements in actual practice? "Prayer must be made without ceasing." "Whatever you ask the Father in my name, it will be given you." *"I am the Life."* [16]

However, the renewal called for by the Council was superficial for some, as Pope Paul VI pointed out early in the post-conciliar era:

...we are aware of the disquiet which agitates certain modern quarters with regard to the faith.... We see even Catholics allowing themselves to be seized by a kind of passion for change and novelty (CPG, 4).

Because of this situation, Paul VI composed a unique document which represents centuries of the Church's solicitude for integrity of doctrine:

> ...that we might give witness to our steadfast will to be faithful to the deposit of the faith which they transmitted to us, and that we might strengthen our desire to live by it in the historical circumstances in which the Church finds herself in her pilgrimage in the midst of the world (CPG, 1).

The Creed of the People of God is the very deposit of faith entrusted by the apostles to their successors and handed on to us in the person of Paul VI.

In response to no. 44 of *Christus Dominus*, The *General Catechetical Directory* was published by the Sacred Congregation for the Clergy in 1971. The purpose is stated in the Foreword:

> The intent of this *Directory* is to provide the basic principles of pastoral theology—these principles have been taken from the Magisterium of the Church, and in a special way from the Second General Vatican Council—by which pastoral action in the ministry of the word can be more fittingly directed and governed.... The theoretical aspect is given primary emphasis.... Such a course of action was adopted especially [because]...the errors which are not infrequently noted in catechesis today can be avoided only if one starts with the correct way of understanding the nature and purposes of catechesis and also the truths which are to be taught by it, with due account being taken of those to whom catechesis is directed and of the conditions in which they live.

The Directory cannot be studied except in the light of those principles which the Magisterium has already established to identify authentic catechesis. The Directory is but one link in the chain of the Church's concern to preserve the deposit of faith intact.

This ever-present concern of the Church is again voiced by Paul VI in *Evangelii nuntiandi*, "On Evangelization in the Modern World." The content of evangelization is, by necessity, the same content as that of catechesis—the deposit of faith—because catechesis is an element of evangelization.

> The Church is the depositary of the Good News to be proclaimed. The promises of the New Alliance in Jesus Christ, the teaching of the Lord and the apostles, the Word of life, the sources of grace and of God's loving kindness, the path of salvation—all these things have been entrusted to her. It is the content of the Gospel, and therefore of evangelization, that she preserves as a precious living heritage, not in order to keep it hidden but to communicate it (EN, 15).

The Apostolic Exhortation *Catechesi tradendae*, "On Catechesis in Our Time," by Pope John Paul II, completes *Evangelii nuntiandi* by its thorough treatment of catechesis. Considering this document as a most recent expression of the Magisterium's constant effort to preserve purity of doctrine, we realize that the Holy Father offers no new methods, no new content. The purpose of this exhortation, the Pope writes, is "to fulfill one of the chief duties of my apostolic ministry" (CT, 4), and it "should strengthen the solidity of the faith and of Christian living..." (CT, 4).

A few passages from this document focus our attention on the Church's continuity of doctrinal content and the source of this content.

Catechesis Is Communion with the Person of Christ

At the heart of catechesis we find, in essence, a Person, the Person of Jesus of Nazareth, "the only Son of the Father...full of grace and truth," who suffered and died for us and who now, after rising, is living with us forever. It is Jesus who is "the way, and the truth, and the life," and Christian living consists in following Christ... (CT, 5).

Transmitting Christ's Teaching

In catechesis it is Christ, the Incarnate Word and Son of God, who is taught—everything else is taught with reference to Him—and it is Christ alone who teaches—anyone else teaches to the extent that he is Christ's spokesman, enabling Christ to teach with his lips (CT, 6).

Specific Aim of Catechesis

The specific aim of catechesis is to develop, with God's help, an as yet initial faith, and to advance in fullness and to nourish day by day the Christian life of the faithful, young and old (CT, 20).

Content of the Message

The one message—the Good News of salvation—that has been heard once or hundreds of times and has been accepted with the heart, is in catechesis probed unceasingly by reflection and systematic study, by awareness of its repercussions on one's personal life—an awareness calling for ever greater commitment—and by inserting it into an organic and harmonious whole, namely, Christian living in society and in the world (CT, 26).

The Source

Catechesis will always draw its content from the living source of the Word of God transmitted in Tradition and the Scriptures, for "Sacred Tradition and Sacred Scripture make up a single sacred deposit of the Word of God, which is entrusted to the Church" (CT, 27).

In a recent address to theologians of Spain,[17] our Holy Father drew attention to a very decisive topic: the essential relationship between theology and faith. Since catechesis and theology are directly related as different forms of the same ministry of the Word (cf. GCD, 17), the point that the Holy Father makes can well be applied to the catechist.

The relationship between theology and faith, the Pope states, "is founded and centered on Christ," and this relationship in turn, "illumines the bond of theology with the Church and with its Magisterium." He continues: "Fidelity to Christ implies, then, faithfulness to the Church which brings with it fidelity to the Magisterium." Then the Holy Father exhorts: "Be faithful to your faith without falling into the dangerous illusion of separating Christ from His Church, or the Church from its Magisterium."

The concern of the Church regarding fidelity to the Magisterium penetrates every aspect of the ministry of the Word. This is so because the Church knows that fidelity to Christ depends on fidelity to the deposit of faith, and she is the guardian and teacher of this deposit.

Father Alberione, too, has developed the thought that the Christian formation of man necessarily takes place in and through the Church of Christ.

The Church, Teacher of faith, morality and prayer, labors to form the perfect Christian, the citizen of heaven. This formation takes place in Christ, who is the Way, the Truth and the Life. He made Himself a Teacher for our sake, and in this elevation, Christianization and divinization of man He is the unique Master. Understanding this clearly, the Church, as the Mystical Body of Jesus Christ, labors wisely to communicate and perfect this education and formation of man, so as to make him a worthy member of Jesus Christ, her Head. She continues His role as an incomparable Teacher.[18]

Christ abides in that Church which He founded on the apostles, and He continues His mission of teaching through her. The Church is infallible in teaching: she is truth. The Church has authority to govern souls: she is way. The Church has power to confer grace through the sacraments: she is life.

FOOTNOTES—CHAPTER FOUR

1. U.S. Bishops, Collective Pastoral Letter, *The Church in Our Day* (Boston: St. Paul Editions, 1968), p. 19.

2. Alberione, *Prediche del Primo Maestro* (Rome: Figlie di San Paolo, 1952-1953), p. 45.

3. *The Didaché*, Ancient Christian Writers, trans. James A. Kleist, S.J. (Westminster, Md: Newman Press, 1948), chap. 11, 1-2.

4. St. Irenaeus, *Proof of the Apostolic Preaching*, Ancient Christian Writers, vol. 16, trans. and annotated by Joseph P. Smith, S.J. (New York: Newman Press, 1952), p. 47.

5. Ibid., p. 108.

6. The Catechumenate is that period of instruction in the whole of Christian life which takes place before Baptism. For a more detailed explanation, see Vatican II's *Decree on the Church's Missionary Activity*, no. 14.

7. St. Irenaeus, *Against the Heresies*, the Ante-Nicene Fathers, vol. 1, Roberts and Donaldson, eds. (Grand Rapids, Mich.: Eerdmans, 1977).

8. St. Cyril of Jerusalem, *Catechesis*, The Fathers of the Church, vol. 61 and 64, trans. McCauley, S.J., and Stephenson (Washington, D.C.: Catholic University of America Press, 1969-1970).

9. Gregory of Nyssa, *The Great Catechism*, The Nicene and Post-Nicene Fathers, vol. V, Schaff and Wace, eds. (Grand Rapids, Mich.: Eerdmans, 1976 reprint), p. 471.

10. St. Augustine, *The First Catechetical Instruction*, Ancient Christian Writers, vol. 2, trans. Rev. Joseph Christopher (Westminster, Md.: Newman Press, 1946), p. 13.

11. Introductory, *Catechism of the Council of Trent*, trans. and annotated by McHugh and Callan (New York: Wagner Inc., 1934), p. 6.

12. Leo XIII, *Taraetsi futura prospicientibus*, p. 18.

13. Pius X, *Acerbo nimis*, p. 7.

14. Pius XI, "Divini illius Magistri," *Education: Papal Teachings*, p. 243.

15. Pope Pius XII, "Allocution to the Assistants of Italian Youth of Catholic Action," *Education: Papal Teachings*, p. 459.

16. Alberione, *Carissimi in San Paolo*, p. 315.

17. Pope John Paul II, "Theologians' Fidelity to Christ Implies Fidelity to the Church and Its Magisterium," *L'Osservatore Romano*, English Weekly Edition, December 20, 1982, p. 4.

18. Alberione, *Carissimi in San Paolo*, p. 673.

Conclusion
"That...I May Live in Them"
(Jn. 17:26)*

While on earth the Divine Master "preached holiness of life to each and every one of His disciples of every condition."[1] Each follower of Christ, each Christian, receives that same invitation: "You must be made perfect as your heavenly Father is perfect" (Mt. 5:48).*

Through Baptism the Christian has become a child of God, a sharer in His divine life. On the day of Baptism we passed from the death of sin to life in Christ (cf. Rom. 6:4). But Baptism is only the beginning of a life that must be directed toward fullness of life in Christ.

> It pleased God to make absolute fullness reside in him and, by means of him, to reconcile everything in his person, both on earth and in the heavens, making peace through the blood of his cross (Col. 1:19-20).*

To achieve this "fullness," the Christian must reproduce the whole Christ in himself, that is, believe the teachings of Christ, follow His example and live His life until he becomes "one in faith and in the knowledge of God's Son, and form[s] that perfect man who is Christ come to full stature" (Eph. 4:13).*

Pope Pius XI wrote:

> The authentic Christian does not renounce the activities of this life, he does not stunt his natural faculties; but he develops and perfects them, by coordinating them with the supernatural.[2]

Father Alberione expresses a similar thought:

> Through natural generation comes the son of man composed of body and soul; from Christian formation comes the son of God, composed of body, soul and grace.[3]

As mentioned in an earlier chapter, Father Alberione understands Christian formation as accomplished through authentic Christian education, and so he writes:

> The formation of the Christian is not a process of acquiring knowledge but a true process of *making*. The result is a "new" being.[4]

To be truly Christian, then, education must form the whole person, mind, will and heart, in the whole Christ, Way, Truth and Life.

Through the centuries the Church has continually called for Christ-centered catechesis, so that man would be able to achieve that "fullness" to which the Lord invites him. The Church has preserved intact the deposit of faith entrusted to her by Jesus Christ through the apostles, and in so doing, she has preserved the "primary and essential object of catechesis...Jesus Christ" (CT, 5).

Authentic catechesis, that is, Christocentric catechesis, will put the person in intimate communication with the Divine Master, the Way, the Truth and the Life, who will lead him to the Father and to a sharing in the life of the Trinity (cf. CT, 5).

If a person is to achieve "fullness" or totality in Christ, knowledge alone is insufficient. Convictions concerning a truth should lead to action so that one *lives* as a follower of Christ (cf. CT, 22). Furthermore, a knowledge of Christ that influences one's actions should also lead to a rich sacramental life with emphasis on the Holy Eucharist because it is here that the Divine Master works in *His* fullness for man's transformation (cf. CT, 23).

Jesus Christ is the *Truth*. Therefore, the Christian should study His doctrine, His thoughts and His judgments, which are contained in the Gospels and in the teachings of His Church. Catechesis, then, should present the principal truths of faith as contained in the articles of the Creed so that the intellect is directed toward Christ.

Jesus Christ is the *Way*. Therefore, the Christian should model his life on that of Christ, and imitate His virtues. To strengthen the will, catechesis should present the commandments and laws of the Church, as well as the virtues of faith, hope and charity, the moral virtues and the beatitudes, as positive means to the enjoyment of happiness.

Jesus Christ is the *Life*. Therefore, the Christian should take every means to grow in grace. Catechesis should point out the means to acquire grace—the sacraments and especially the Holy

Eucharist—so that the Christian will have all the possibilities of growing in the supernatural life of grace. Liturgical prayer and private prayer should be presented as the means for the soul to express its adoration and thanksgiving. The sentiments of the heart are then directed toward love for God.

Father Alberione views fullness of life in Christ as "configuration":

> This configuration signifies total and complete donation of ourselves—in our physical, moral and intellectual powers, as well as in the very being from which these powers come.
>
> It means taking the whole Master in His light, in His spirit, in His examples and in His grace. Live in Him, for Him, with Him and from Him.[5]

Because the Way, Truth and Life method is in essence Christocentric, if implemented correctly in catechetics, it will form the whole person in the whole Christ. Thus the Christian will reach that fullness of life in Christ to which he has been called. Through doctrine, morality and prayer, catechesis is able to form the intellectual, behavioral and emotional levels of the Christian so that his mind, will and heart are centered on Christ. He will gradually become, in fact, "another Christ," as St. Paul expressed it:

> The life I live now is not my own; Christ is living in me. I still live my human life, but it is a life of faith in the Son of God (Gal. 2:20).*

FOOTNOTES—CONCLUSION

1. Vatican Council II, "Lumen gentium," *The Conciliar and Post Conciliar Documents*, general ed Austin Flannery, O.P. (Boston: St. Paul Editions, 1981). no. 40.
2. Pius XI, "Divini illius Magistri," *Education: Papal Teachings*, p. 245.
3. Alberione, *Meditation on Christian Formation*, Haec Meditare, Serie Prima, vol. IV.
4. Ibid.
5. Alberione, *Gesù Maestro*, Haec Meditare, Serie Prima, vol. III.

BIBLIOGRAPHY—BOOKS

Alberione, James J., S.S.P., S.T.D. *Abundantes Divitiae Gratiae Suae*. Rome: Pious Society of St. Paul, 1979, translated and printed by the Daughters of St. Paul, Boston, 1979.

———. *Alle Famiglie Paoline*. Rome: Edizioni Paoline, 1954. English translation: *To the Pauline Families* by the Daughters of St. Paul, Boston, 1954.

———. *Carissimi in San Paolo*. Edited by Rosario F. Esposito, S.S.P. Rome: Edizioni Paoline, 1971.

———. *Haec Meditare*, vol. III. Alba, Italy: Figlie di San Paolo, 1947.

———. *Haec Meditare*, vol. IV. Alba, Italy: Figlie di San Paolo, 1948-1949.

———. *Pauline Spirituality*. Translated and printed by the Daughters of St. Paul, Boston, 1974.

———. *Personality and Configuration With Christ*. Boston: St. Paul Editions, 1967.

———. *Santificazione della Mente*. Rome: Edizioni Paoline, 1956. English translation: *Sanctification of the Mind* by the Daughters of St. Paul, Boston.

Augustine, St. *The First Catechetical Instruction*. Ancient Christian Writers Series, vol. 2. Translated by Joseph P. Christopher, Ph.D. Edited by Johannes Quasten, S.T.D. and Joseph C. Plumpe, Ph.D. Westminster, Md.: The Newman Press, 1946.

Aumann, Jordan, O.P. *Spiritual Theology*. Huntington, Ind.: Our Sunday Visitor, Inc., and London: Sheed and Ward, 1979.

Bonivento, Cesare, PIME (Coordinator). *"Going, Teach..."*: Commentary on the Apostolic Exhortation *Catechesi tradendae* of John Paul II. Boston: St. Paul Editions, 1980.

Catechism of the Council of Trent for Parish Priests. Translated by Rev. John A. McHugh, O.P., and Rev. Charles J. Callan, O.P. New York: Joseph F. Wagner, Inc., 1934.

Cyril of Jerusalem, St. "Catecheses 13-18, Mystagogical Lectures, etc." *The Works of Saint Cyril of Jerusalem*, vol. 2. Fathers of the Church Series, vol. 64. Translated by Leo P. McCauley, S.J., and Anthony A. Stephenson. Editorial Director, Bernard M. Peebles. Washington, D.C.: Catholic University of America Press, Inc., 1970.

——————. "Procatechesis, Catecheses, 1-12." *The Works of Saint Cyril of Jerusalem*, vol. 1. Fathers of the Church Series, vol. 61. Translated by Leo P. McCauley, S.J., and Anthony A. Stephenson. Editorial Director, Roy Joseph Deferrari. Washington, D.C.: Catholic University of America Press, Inc., 1969.

Damino, Andrea, S.S.P. *Bibliografia di Don Giacomo Alberione*. Rome: Edizioni dell'Archivio Storico Generale della Famiglia Paolina, 1979.

Daughters of St. Paul, eds. *Catechism of Modern Man*. Boston: St. Paul Editions, 1968.

The Didaché. Ancient Christian Writers, vol. 6. Translated by James A. Kleist, S.J. Westminster, Md.: Newman Press, 1948.

Donceel, J., S.J. *Philosophical Psychology*. New York: Sheed and Ward, 1955.

Flannery, Austin, O.P. general ed. *Vatican Council II: the Conciliar and Post Conciliar Documents*. Boston: St. Paul Editions, 1981.

Frumento, Gianfranco, S.S.P. *La Catechesi nei Documenti della Santa Sede*. Rome: Edizioni Paoline, 1965.

Gannon, Timothy. *Psychology: The Unity of Human Behavior*. Boston: Ginn and Company, 1954.

Giaccardo, Timoteo D., S.S.P. *Dai Tetti In Su*. Rome: Edizioni Paoline, 1956.

Gregory of Nyssa. Select Writings and Letters of, in Schaff-Wace (eds.) *Nicene and Post-Nicene Fathers of the Christian Church*, Second Series, vol. V. Grand Rapids, Michigan: Eerdmans Publishing Co., 1976, reprint.

Hofinger, Johannes, S.J., and Buckley, Francis J., S.J. *The Good News and Its Proclamation*. Notre Dame, Ind : University of Notre Dame Press, 1968.

Irenaeus, St. "Against Heresies" in *The Apostolic Fathers with Justin Martyr and Irenaeus*, vol. 1. Roberts-Donaldson (eds.) Grand Rapids, Michigan: Eerdmans Publishing Co., 1977, reprint.

_____. *Proof of the Apostolic Preaching*. Ancient Christian Writers, vol. 16. Translated by Joseph P. Smith, S.J. Edited by Johannes Quasten, S.T.D., and Joseph C. Plumpe, Ph.D. New York: Newman Press, 1952.

Jerusalem Bible, The. Garden City, N. Y.: Doubleday and Company, 1968.

Jungmann, Joseph A. *Handing on the Faith*. New York: Herder and Herder, 1962.

Kevane, Msgr. Eugene. *Creed and Catechetics*. Westminster, Md.: Christian Classics, 1977.

_____, ed. *Teaching the Catholic Faith Today*. Documents of the Holy See. Introduction and Topical Index by Rev. Msgr. Eugene Kevane. Boston: St. Paul Editions, 1982.

Lamera, Stefano, S.S.P. *Gesù Maestro, Via, Verità e Vita*. Alba, Italy: Edizioni Paoline, 1949.

Neuner, Josef, S.J., and Dupuis, J., S.J., eds. *The Christian Faith in the Doctrinal Documents of the Catholic Church*. Westminster, Md.: Christian Classics, Inc., 1975.

New American Bible, The. Paterson, N.J.: St. Anthony Guild Press, 1970

Ott, Ludwig. *Fundamentals of Catholic Dogma*. Rockford, Il.: Tan Books and Publishers, Inc., 1974.

Roatta, Giovanni., S.S.P., *Gesù Maestro*. Alba, Italy: Edizioni Paoline, 1955.

Robaldo, Rev. Giovanni, S.S.P., *Il Divin Maestro*. Rome: Edizioni Paoline, 1961.

Royo, Antonio M., and Aumann, Jordan. *The Theology of Christian Perfection*. Dubuque, Iowa: Priory Press, 1962.

Solesmes, Benedictine Monks of, eds. *Education: Papal Teachings*. Boston: St. Paul Editions, 1960.

BIBLIOGRAPHY—DOCUMENTS

Bishops of the United States. *The Church in Our Day.* Collective Pastoral Letter. Boston: St. Paul Editions, 1968.

Documents of Vatican Council I. Selected and translated by John F. Broderick, S.J. Collegeville, Mn.: Liturgical Press, 1971.

John Paul II, Pope. Apostolic Exhortation *Catechesi tradendae.* Boston: St. Paul Editions, 1979.

——————. *Redemptor hominis* [The Redeemer of Man]. Boston: St. Paul Editions, 1979.

Leo XIII, Pope. *Aeterni Patris* [On the Restoration of Christian Philosophy]. Boston: St. Paul Editions, 1979.

——————. *Tametsi futura prospicientibus* [On Jesus Christ Our Redeemer]. Boston: St. Paul Editions, 1979.

National Conference of Catholic Bishops. *Basic Teachings for Catholic Religious Education.* Washington, D.C.: U S.C.C., 1973.

——————. *To Teach As Jesus Did.* Washington, D.C.: U.S.C.C., 1973.

Paul VI, Pope. Apostolic Exhortation *Evangelii nuntiandi* [On Evangelization in the Modern World]. Boston: St. Paul Editions, 1975.

Pius X, Pope. *Acervo nimis* [On the Teaching of Christian Doctrine]. Translated by Joseph B. Collins, S.S., D.D., Ph.D. Boston: St. Paul Editions, 1979.

———————. *Pascendi Dominici gregis* [On the Doctrine of the Modernists] and *Lamentabili sane* [Syllabus Condemning the Errors of the Modernists]. Boston: St. Paul Editions, 1977.

Pius XII, Pope. *Humani generis*. Translated by N.C.W.C. Boston: St. Paul Editions, 1956.

Pontifical Biblical Commission. *The Historicity of the Gospels*. Boston: St. Paul Editions, 1981.

Sacred Congregation for the Clergy. The *General Catechetical Directory*. Washington, D.C.: U.S.C.C., 1971.

Prayers for the Catechist

To Jesus Master

1. Jesus, Divine Master, we adore You as the Word Incarnate *sent* by the Father to instruct men in life-giving truths. You are uncreated *Truth*, the only Master. You alone have words of eternal life. We thank You for having ignited in us the light of reason and the light of faith, and for having called us to the light of glory. We believe, submitting our whole mind to You and to the Church; and we condemn all that the Church condemns. Master, show us the treasures of Your wisdom, let us know the Father, make us Your true disciples. Increase our faith so that we may attain to the eternal vision in heaven.

Jesus Master, Way and Truth and Life, have mercy on us.

2. Jesus, Divine Master, we adore You as the *Beloved* of the Father, the sole *Way* to Him. We thank You because You made Yourself our model. You left us examples of the highest perfection. You have invited men to follow You on earth and in heaven. We contemplate You in the various periods of Your earthly life. We docilely place ourselves in Your school and condemn every moral which differs from Yours. Draw us to You so that by following in Your footsteps and renouncing ourselves, we may seek only Your will. Increase

active hope in us and the desire to be found similar to You at the judgment, and to possess You forever in heaven.

Jesus Master, etc.

3. Jesus, Divine Master, we adore You as the *only-begotten Son* of God, come on the earth to give *Life*, the most abundant Life, to man. We thank You because, by dying on the cross, You merited life for us, which You give us in Baptism and nourish in Holy Communion and in the other sacraments. Live in us, O Jesus, with the outpouring of the Holy Spirit, so that we may love You with our whole mind, strength, and heart, and love our neighbor as ourselves for love of You. Increase charity in us, so that one day, called from the sepulcher to the glorious life, we may be united with You in the eternal happiness of heaven.

Jesus Master, etc.

4. Jesus, Divine Master, we adore You living in the Church, Your Mystical Body, and our sole ark of salvation. We thank You for having given us this infallible and indefectible Mother, in whom You continue to be for man the Way, the Truth and the Life. We ask of You that all the non-Christians may come to her inextinguishable light, the erring return to her, and all mankind be united in faith, in a common hope, in charity. Exalt the Church, assist the Pope, sanctify the priests and the souls consecrated to You. Lord Jesus, our wish is Yours: that there be one fold under one Shepherd, so that we may all be reunited in the Church triumphant in heaven.

Jesus Master, etc.

5. Jesus, Divine Master, we adore You with the angels who sang the reasons for Your Incarnation: "Glory to God and peace to men." We thank You for having called us to share in Your own apostolate. Enkindle in us Your own flame of zeal for God and for souls. Fill all our powers with Yourself. Live in us so that we may radiate You through the apostolate of prayer and suffering, of editions and of word, of example and of deeds. Send good laborers into Your vineyard. Enlighten preachers, teachers, writers; infuse in them the Holy Spirit with His seven gifts; dispose minds and hearts to receive Him. Come, Master and Lord! Teach and reign, through Mary, Mother, Teacher and Queen.

Jesus Master, etc.

Invocations to Jesus Master

Jesus Master, sanctify my mind and increase my faith.

Jesus, teaching in the Church, draw everyone to Your school.

Jesus Master, deliver me from error, from vain thoughts, and from eternal darkness.

O Jesus, Way between the Father and us, I offer You all and await all from You.

O Jesus, Way of sanctity, make me Your faithful imitator.

O Jesus Way, render me perfect as the Father who is in heaven.

O Jesus Life, live in me, so that I may live in You.

O Jesus Life, do not permit me to separate myself from You.

O Jesus Life, grant that I may live eternally in the joy of Your love.

O Jesus Truth, may I be light for the world.

O Jesus Way, may I be example and model for souls.

O Jesus Life, may my presence bring grace and consolation everywhere.

To Read Sacred Scripture

Before reading Sacred Scripture

O Jesus Christ, our Master, You are the Way, and the Truth, and the Life. Grant that we may learn the supereminent knowledge of Your charity in the spirit of St. Paul the Apostle and of the Catholic Church. Send Your Holy Spirit to teach us and remind us of what You preached.

Jesus Master, Way and Truth and Life, have mercy on us.

After reading Sacred Scripture

Jesus, Divine Master, You have words of eternal life.

I believe, O Lord and *Truth,* but increase my faith.

I love You, O Lord and *Way,* with all my strength, because You have commanded us to observe Your commandments perfectly.

I pray to You, O Lord and *Life;* I adore You, I praise You, I beseech You, and I thank You for the gift of Sacred Scripture.

With Mary, I shall remember and preserve Your words in my mind and I shall meditate on them in my heart.

Jesus Master, Way and Truth and Life, have mercy on us.

Those who devoutly read Sacred Scripture as spiritual reading gain a partial indulgence. If the reading lasts at least a half hour, the indulgence will be plenary.

The Daughters of St. Paul

It has been said that if St. Paul were to return to the earth, he would use the modern and efficacious means of communication to preach the Word of God.

In 1953, His Holiness, Pope Pius XII, blessed, praised and approved the modern congregation, the Pious Society of the *Daughters of St. Paul,* which is dedicated to the spreading of the Faith by using the apostolate of the press, radio, television and motion pictures, as St. Paul, their father, would have done.

These modern media are a most effective means of reaching souls. They have become a terrible weapon in the hands of Satan; they must be a powerful sword and shield for the Church to promote the kingdom of Jesus Christ.

The Daughters of St. Paul offer their daily prayers, sacrifices and labor in reparation for the sins committed through bad literature, films and programs, and they endeavor to replace these with *good,* wholesome literature, films, TV and radio programs. These Sisters write, print, bind, broadcast and film the Word of God.

The literature from their presses as well as their films are distributed by the Sisters themselves through their *St. Paul Catholic Book and Film Centers* and also by "house-to-house" distribution—a technique they know has never failed, the very technique their patron, St. Paul, employed.

The Daughters of St. Paul carry out their important apostolate in 32 nations. Their congregation is young—founded in 1915 by Very Reverend James Alberione, S.S.P., S.T.D., and their Co-Foundress, the Servant of God, Mother Thecla Merlo. St. Paul, the Apostle, is their Protector. In imitation of him, therefore, the Daughters of St. Paul strive to zealously and generously dedicate all their energies to the work of sanctifying themselves and winning many souls to God.

Daughters of St. Paul

IN MASSACHUSETTS
  50 St. Paul's Ave., Jamaica Plain, Boston, MA 02130; **617-522-8911**.
  172 Tremont Street, Boston, MA 02111; **617-426-5464; 617-426-4230**.
IN NEW YORK
  78 Fort Place, Staten Island, NY 10301; **212-447-5071; 212-447-5086**.
  59 East 43rd Street, New York, NY 10017; **212-986-7580**.
  625 East 187th Street, Bronx, NY 10458; **212-584-0440**.
  525 Main Street, Buffalo, NY 14203; **716-847-6044**.
IN NEW JERSEY
  Hudson Mall—Route 440 and Communipaw Ave.,
    Jersey City, NJ 07304; **201-433-7740**.
IN CONNECTICUT
  202 Fairfield Ave., Bridgeport, CT 06604; **203-335-9913**.
IN OHIO
  2105 Ontario Street (at Prospect Ave.), Cleveland, OH 44115;
    216-621-9427.
  25 E. Eighth Street, Cincinnati, OH 45202; **513-721-4838;
    513-421-5733**.
IN PENNSYLVANIA
  1719 Chestnut Street, Philadelphia, PA 19103; **215-568-2638**.
IN VIRGINIA
  1025 King Street, Alexandria, VA 22314; **703-683-1741; 703-549-3806**.
IN FLORIDA
  2700 Biscayne Blvd., Miami, FL 33137; **305-573-1618**.
IN LOUISIANA
  4403 Veterans Memorial Blvd., Metairie, LA 70002; **504-887-7631;
    504-887-0113**.
  1800 South Acadian Thruway, P.O. Box 2028, Baton Rouge, LA 70821;
    504-343-4057; 504-381-9485.
IN MISSOURI
  1001 Pine Street (at North 10th), St. Louis, MO 63101; **314-621-0346;
    314-231-1034**.
IN ILLINOIS
  172 North Michigan Ave., Chicago, IL 60601; **312-346-4228;
    312-346-3240**.
IN TEXAS
  114 Main Plaza, San Antonio, TX 78205; **512-224-8101; 512-224-0938**.
IN CALIFORNIA
  1570 Fifth Ave., San Diego, CA 92101; **619-232-1442**.
  46 Geary Street, San Francisco, CA 94108; **415-781-5180**.
IN WASHINGTON
  2301 Second Ave., Seattle, WA 98121.
IN HAWAII
  1143 Bishop Street, Honolulu, HI 96813; **808-521-2731**.
IN ALASKA
  750 West 5th Ave., Anchorage, AK 99501; **907-272-8183**.

IN CANADA
  3022 Dufferin Street, Toronto 395, Ontario, Canada.

IN ENGLAND
  199 Kensington High Street, London W8 63A, England.
  133 Corporation Street Birmingham B4 6PH, England.
  5A-7 Royal Exchange Square, Glasgow G1 3AH, England.
  82 Bold Street, Liverpool L1 4HR, England.

IN AUSTRALIA
  58 Abbotsford Rd., Homebush, N.S.W. 2140, Australia.